craft your own cosy scandi christmas

GIFT IDEAS, CRAFT PROJECTS AND RECIPES FOR FESTIVE HYGGE

craft your own cosy scandi christmas

GIFT IDEAS, CRAFT PROJECTS AND RECIPES FOR FESTIVE HYGGE

BECCI COOMBES

WHITE OWL

AN IMPRINT OF PEN & SWORD BOOKS LTD.
YORKSHIRE – PHILADELPHIA

First published in Great Britain in 2022 by
Pen & Sword WHITE OWL
An imprint of
Pen & Sword Books Ltd
Yorkshire – Philadelphia

ISBN 9781399093842

A CIP catalogue record for this book is
available from the British Library.

Printed and bound in the UK, by Short Run Press Limited, Exeter.

Photography by Becci Coombes
Design: Paul Wilkinson

Pen & Sword Books Limited incorporates the imprints of Atlas, Archaeology, Aviation, Discovery, Family History, Fiction, History, Maritime, Military, Military Classics, Politics, Select, Transport, True Crime, Air World, Frontline Publishing, Leo Cooper, Remember When, Seaforth Publishing, The Praetorian Press, Wharncliffe Local History, Wharncliffe Transport, Wharncliffe True Crime and White Owl.

For a complete list of Pen & Sword titles please contact:
PEN & SWORD BOOKS LIMITED
47 Church Street, Barnsley, South Yorkshire, S70 2AS, England
E-mail: enquiries@pen-and-sword.co.uk
Website: www.pen-and-sword.co.uk

Or
PEN AND SWORD BOOKS
1950 Lawrence Rd, Havertown, PA 19083, USA
E-mail: Uspen-and-sword@casematepublishers.com
Website: www.penandswordbooks.com

CONTENTS

ACKNOWLEDGEMENTS

Once again, I am indebted to friends and family for their love and support as they were constantly asked to test recipes, eat brownies or compare gnomes. My dear Mummy, Gem, Lou, Katie, Sarah, Angela, Heather, Sue, Tim, Nessy, Vic, Dan B., Elsie and Alex; thank you all so much for your help. Massive love to the Coombes family too, for answering the siren call of herring and the schnapps bell over the years, while Noah and Vince are the best super models an aunt could have. Sada helped me style the rice pudding (not an easy task) and Jane also deserves huge thanks for starting me off on the fabulous roller-coaster of writing. Dan W. merits a special mention for his love, help and having to listen to me interminably bang on about everything from the manufacture of Scandinavian paint to rye bread texture, and my cousin Claus was kind enough to endure many phone calls on the niceties of Danish grammar. I am also eternally grateful to my grandmothers for teaching me to cook, crochet, paint and be creative, and to my grandfather who taught me to try and be patient even when things aren't going quite as well as I planned.

Huge thanks are due to everyone at White Owl for giving me the opportunity to write this book, and for all the fun I have had doing so.

Lastly, the biggest love goes to my son Wolf (chief recipe tester) and the cat, who has engaged in every craft project in this book with great enthusiasm, particularly when it involves yarn, ribbon, sewing thread or string.

ABOUT THE AUTHOR

Becci grew up with a love for all things Scandinavian. Originally she trained as an archaeologist (Vikings, of course), before travelling the world and becoming a successful glass artist. She now runs www.hyggestyle.co.uk, an online boutique specialising in Danish and Scandinavian gifts, homewares, recipe and craft ideas. She is also a youth group leader, teaches bushcraft, foraging and survival to local teenagers. She lives with her son, cat and chickens, and loves herring and sci-fi.

Hearts and baubles.

INTRODUCTION

For the last few years hygge (pronounced hoo-gah), has become a byword for cosiness and is often associated with socks, candles and a luxurious fluffy blanket. While all these accessories can definitely contribute to a hyggelig feeling, it is not necessarily a definition that Danes would recognise. Hygge, in Denmark, is more about a sense of connection: warmth, family and friendship, whether gathered around a table for a meal together or sharing a flask of cocoa on a really otherwise quite miserable drizzly walk.

I think that most people have always experienced the concept of hygge, even if they didn't know the name for it: family roasts, Sunday walks, rainy afternoons with board games and cake … all these embody that special feeling. And no season says hygge quite like Christmas, with its emphasis on sparkling lights, twinkling candles, festive comfort food and time with loved ones.

Denmark at Christmas is one of the most magical places on Earth. Crowds stroll gently through fairy-lit markets, sipping mulled wine, breath frosting in the night air, and gathering around fire pits to sample æbleskiver dumplings and jam. Illuminated paper stars glow in every window, welcoming the weary traveller home through the long dark winter nights, to enjoy long, convivial family feasts.

As a child, I was taught traditional Danish recipes and crafts by my grandmother (having been forced to curtsy, most resentfully, to her first) and childhood holidays were spent at the family farm on the island of Sjælland. Long golden summers were whiled

Shoppers enjoying a stroll through Tivoli Gardens, Copenhagen.

away playing in the dark pine forests and on the white sandy beaches, but Christmas was a time for cutting paper decorations, baking, and singing carols, and trying to discreetly lose bags of pungent salted liquorice that were given to us at every house we visited.

Even though we no longer spend all our winter holidays in Denmark, we still carry on the traditions with which I grew up, celebrating Christmas Eve by lighting candles in the garden for the reindeer to find our house, cooking roast pork and red cabbage and then enjoying a good-natured squabble over a game or two. Here, then, are the recipes my family love most, along with ideas for crafts and gifts to help bring a little festive hygge to your home. At this point, I feel I must come clean and make it clear that I am not in any way a trained chef (my courgette soup is notoriously unpleasant) so I invite you to use these recipes as a starting point for your own family traditions and please tweak them as you see fit. I would also add that all ovens have their own idiosyncrasies (mine being particularly prone to unexpected eccentricity), so if you know yours runs particularly hot, please adjust the temperatures accordingly.

The author being forced by her mother to pose as The Little Mermaid on Vemmetofte Strand.

This is the second book I have written during a lockdown, and, as such, necessity demanded that I had to forage, both in woodland and wardrobe, for many of the elements for these projects. As a result, I was loath to throw away any materials that were left over, so a number of the ideas have a few extra creations that can be made with any surplus. Some of the materials I had to buy online, so you will notice that ingredients in the home-made gift section pop up repeatedly so as little as possible is wasted; bicarbonate of soda is used in everything from clay ornaments to bath salts, while cinnamon becomes both a spiced winter tea and a table centrepiece. I hope you have fun making them, and wish you the most hyggelig of festive seasons!

A cabin selling gløgg.

CHAPTER ONE

DECORATING FOR CHRISTMAS

The concept of Scandinavian home style is very much based on a pared-back feel, with white walls, neutral accents and clean lines. This originated from the mid-twentieth century, when property prices were high and living spaces compact as a result; furniture thus had to take the place of both functional item and ornament. Resulting in the spare aesthetic we now think of as Nordic style, it is accentuated by the use of natural wood, both for furniture and floors, a variety of textures (think sheepskin rugs and cable knit throws) and the occasional touches of nature, such as the vibrant greenery of houseplants or a clear glass vase full of bare twigs.

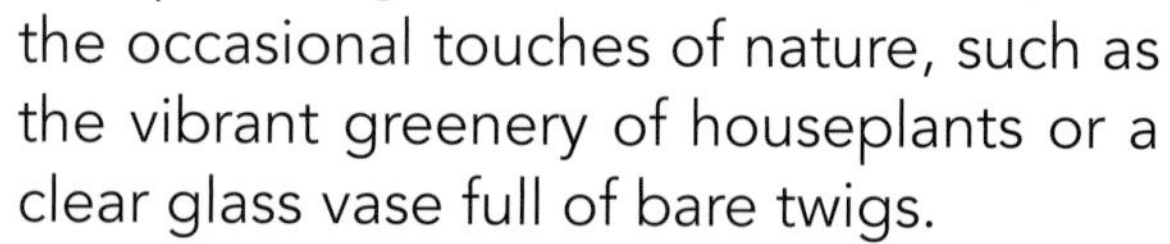

However, at Christmas all this 'form over function' business is thrown well out of the window, as families decorate every available surface with iconic Danish ornaments. Red woven hearts adorn everything from shopping streets to Christmas trees, while most homes will have white candle arches in every window to greet visitors. Fairy lights tend to be a warm white, rather than multi-coloured, and many families still follow the tradition of having real candles burning on their tree on Christmas Eve.

The tradition I love most is that of the *nisser* or elves, figures from Danish folklore that live in farm buildings and are reputed to take care of both the home and the livestock. Slightly short of temper, they are helpful when treated well, but woe betide anyone who takes them for

My Christmas tree

granted. Many people still leave out a bowl of rice pudding on Christmas Eve (elves love it served with butter), so the nisser don't tie the tails of their cows together or hide everyone's shoes. These little fellows can be found everywhere at Christmas, dressed in red and grey woollens and their signature red pointy hats.

As Danes famously know, there is nothing like the warmth and friendly glow of a flame to add a little magic to your home, especially at Christmas, so here are a few handy tips to ensure you get the best from your precious candles:

1. When lighting them for the first time, allow to burn for long enough so the wax melts across the whole surface. This prevents tunnelling (where the flame burns down just in the centre of the candle, leading to wasted wax) and will extend their life.

2. Keep the wick trimmed down to about 5mm as this should also help an even burn and prevent any soot. If your candle has more than one wick, make sure they are all the same length.

3. If you really want to show your candle some love, don't blow it out. To extinguish the flame, poke the wick down into the melted wax with a pair of tweezers and then lift it out again; this stops any soot forming and helps keep the scent pure.

4. Try placing the candle low down in the room, for example in the fireplace rather than on the mantelpiece. Scent rises, so if your candle is placed higher up you will be losing much of the fragrance.

5. It goes without saying that candles should always be burnt on a flat surface and away from any draughts. Keep away from children and pets, never leave them burning unattended and don't let them burn down further than the bottom 1cm of wax.

LARGE RUSTIC SILVER BIRCH WREATH

A stroll through the woods after high winds or a heavy winter storm can provide all sorts of materials for foraged decorations. This striking wreath was made from fallen silver birch twigs in a local nature reserve, and after a quick word with the ranger, he was happy for me to take as much as I liked. I also found a few pieces of birch bark that were lying on the path so snaffled those as well (don't pull

bark off the tree as it can leave it open to infection).

The base for the wreath was made with green willow withies twisted into a ring, which can be cut in winter when the tree is free from leaves. If you are gathering them this way, bring them indoors for a few hours to warm up before you start to work as they will be much easier to bend.

Withies can also be bought online, and you can get a large bundle delivered quite cheaply, which will last through lots of seasonal projects; I use Somerset willow, which is grown traditionally and harvested sustainably from large wetland beds on the Somerset Levels. In the winter, green willow is available and this will not need soaking, but the rest of the year it may need to be immersed in water to make it supple.

For this large wreath, I used a willow base measuring approximately 40cm, and bundles of twigs that were between 50cm and 60cm in length. The design was fairly simple with only a few bark hearts for embellishment giving a wild woodland feel; however, the whole structure is quite forgiving so you can slide in any berry sprigs or sprays of greenery as the mood takes you.

Materials (for a wreath measuring just over a metre in diameter)

- 6 willow withies or a ready-made wreath (a seven-foot long stem should give a lovely round form at least 30–40cm in diameter)
- Bundle of birch twigs
- Birch bark
- Floristry reel wire
- Garden twine
- Scissors
- Secateurs
- Hot glue gun

1. To make the willow base, hold the cut end of one of the withies in your left hand and bend it round, looping it into the size of wreath you desire.

2. Wind the tip around the back and then weave it round and round the form, heading to the right. Tuck the end in to secure.

3. Turn your wreath roughly 60 degrees to the left, and repeat; stick the cut end in from front to back towards the left, leaving a little tail sticking out, then continue to wrap the tip around until you can go no further. Keep turning the wreath to the left, inserting a new withy, and then winding the tip to the right.

4. After you have woven in six withies, you should be back roughly where you started. Now you can apply a little pressure where needed, gently easing the willow into a circular shape. When you are happy with it, snip the ends and tips off, always holding your secateurs at the same angle to make it look neat.

5. Tie a piece of twine around the top of your wreath to make a hanging loop.

6. Attach the reel of floristry wire to the base, then place a bundle of twigs on top and wrap the wire round the stems and base tightly a few times. Ensure the twiggy ends are poking out at an angle as this will give a lovely diffuse edge to the project; don't worry if the thicker end is poking out as well, as these will also be wired in later.

7. Lay another bundle of twigs over the first bunch so they cover the stems and then wire tightly again.

8. Repeat this all the way round, making sure you pull on the wire quite hard so it pulls the cut ends into the base, making it thicker and stronger.

9. When you reach the beginning, push the last cut stems underneath the first twiggy ends and wire them on at the back, finishing the wreath off neatly.

10. Trim off any little sections that require tidying up. At this stage it is also very simple to fill in any gaps; simply cut smaller sections and slip them in between the twig stems and the wire.

11. If it is quite dry and grubby, your bark may need cleaning before you can work with it. Soak it in water for 1–2 hours until flexible, and then scrub off any debris with a pan scourer.

12. While the bark is still damp, cut out hearts, stars or any other design you fancy using a sharp pair of scissors, then leave to dry thoroughly (hot glue won't adhere properly if the bark is still damp, and they may drop off when you least expect it).

13. Add a blob of hot glue to the back of each heart and fix in place around the edges of the wreath. Any willow trimmings can easily be cut into 6cm sections and glued together to make little reindeer. Add some twiggy antlers and brush with white chalk paint as a festive addition to your mantelpiece.

DECOUPAGE ADVENT CANDLE

Lighting Advent candles is an important tradition in the lead-up to Christmas. Many families will have a wreath with four candles, each one being lit in turn on the Sundays in December, but children particularly love lighting a special candle at breakfast. Marked with the twenty-four days of Advent, it can be a quiet moment of calm in an otherwise hectic month, as you all sit and wait for it to burn down to the next number. Making your own Advent candle is easy and just requires a few household items and a little imagination; add your family's names and the year for a personalised ornament.

The fact that a wide pillar is used here rather than a taper candle means that the tissue should never be too close to the flame as to present a hazard. As with all candles, ensure it is placed on a fireproof surface, never leave it unattended while burning and keep the wick trimmed to 5mm.

Materials

- White tissue paper
- White baking parchment
- 20cm white pillar candle
- Hairdryer
- Felt tip pens
- Masking tape

1. Draw your design on a piece of white paper (ensuring it will fit on your candle). An easy way to do this is to print out a vertical column of numbers and then pen your illustration around them.

2. Cut a piece of tissue paper and, placing it over the top, trace the image using felt tip pens.

3. Carefully trim round your design with scissors.

4. Place the tissue on to the candle, and then tape a piece of baking parchment around it so the

1
2
3
4
5
6
7
8
9
10
11
12
13
14
15
16
17
18
19
20
21
22
23
24

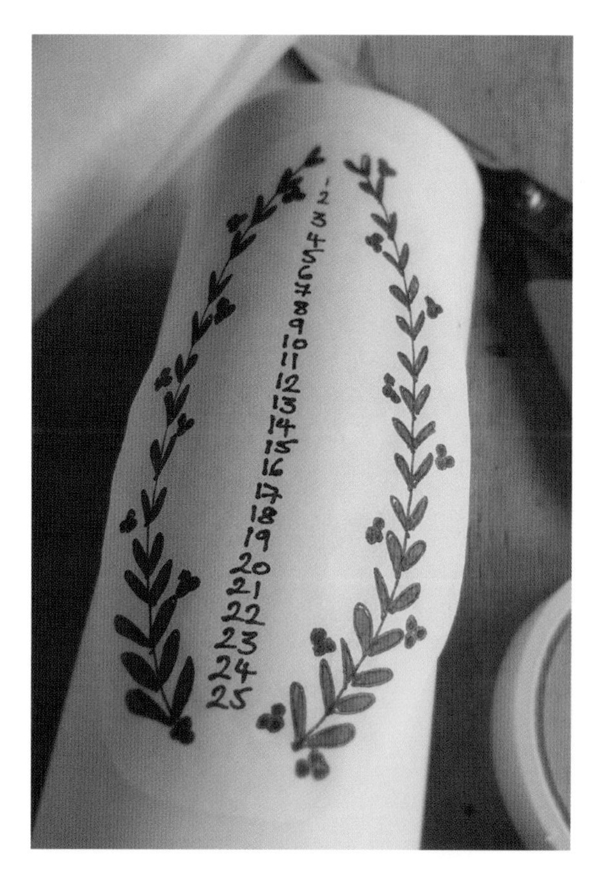

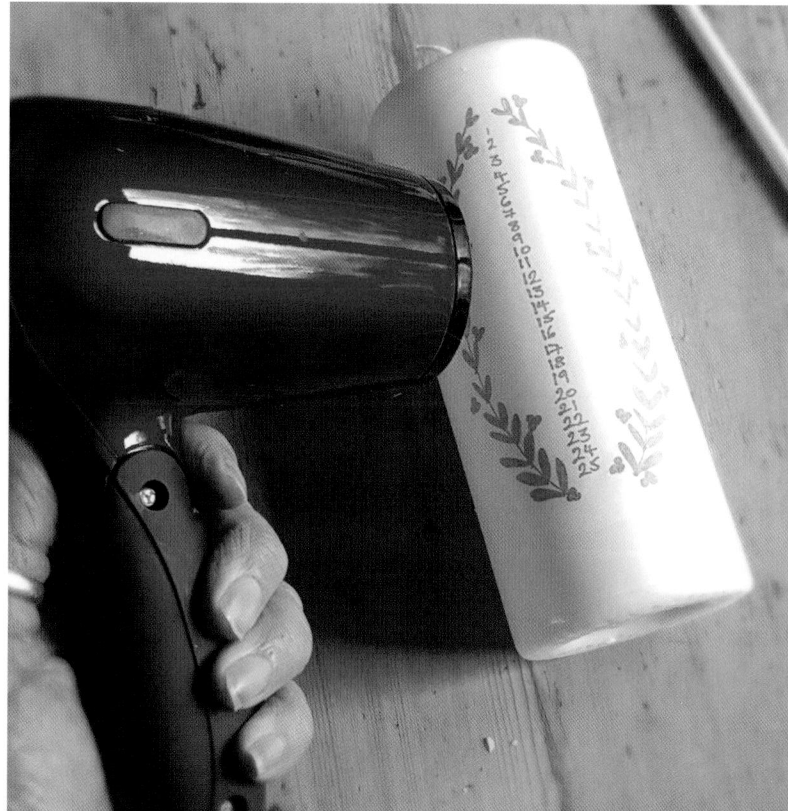

design is held down firmly. Make sure the waxy side of the baking paper is facing the candle.

5. Using the hairdryer, apply heat evenly across the baking parchment. As the wax starts to soften, it will seep into the tissue and bond it to the candle (using white parchment allows you to see which areas have melted and which still need more heat).

6. Gently remove the parchment, giving any areas which are still not quite glued on another quick blast with the hairdryer and gently pushing them down.

7. Once you have mastered the knack, this technique can be used to make all kinds of wonderful personalised candles, from wedding table numbers to anniversary gifts. You can also use pretty patterned 3-ply napkins by carefully peeling away the top layer and discarding the bottom two, before continuing with the above method.

JULESTJERNER CHANDELIER

Julestjerner (Danish paper woven stars) are an iconic sight in Scandinavia during the festive season, and can be seen hanging in windows and embellishing every Christmas tree. Taught to make them when I was small, I still find the weaving and folding very therapeutic, and their pretty geometric designs look wonderful

either hanging on cotton from your tree or piled up in glass bowls with a few twinkling lights.

This festive chandelier was the result of staring blankly at the ceiling and wondering how I could make a julestjerner mobile that incorporated fairy lights. The result is a hanging wreath, which, with its touches of greenery and warm white glow, would look lovely suspended over a Christmas table. I like to remove the pine when it has become unattractively crispy and replace it with a few sprigs of herbs, but a few silver birch twigs wired on also look wonderful.

Paper star strips are available to purchase online, but you can easily make them yourself from sheets of wrapping paper or wall paper. Firstly, iron your paper if necessary so it lies beautifully flat, then using a guillotine or paper cutter, mark and cut the strips so that the length is thirty times the width. A 1cm wide strip therefore needs to be 30cm long, and will give you a star roughly four times the width (so 4cm in this case). Fold the strips in half and crease well, then you are ready to start.

There are a couple of tips which make the weaving process easier if you have never tried it before; firstly snipping the end of the strips at an angle makes them easier to push through the slots. Secondly, if the end of your strip becomes crumpled, cut that off too as you will have little chance of being able to weave it if it loses its rigidity.

Micro fairy lights are tiny LEDs set into thin wire which are usually available in either a silver or copper colour, and have the handy property of both being very flexible and holding their shape to some extent. Try and choose a set where the battery pack has a hanging loop, then it can be suspended from your ceiling hook and disguised with a few more pine sprigs. I also cannot stress enough how important it is to not unroll the lights until you start wrapping the wire around the chandelier, no matter how excited you are to start the project; I got myself into an absolute mess by having a quick experimental fiddle with them before I started and therefore heartily recommend being patient. It is also much easier to attach the stars to the wire drops once the chandelier is already hanging, so you may wish to organise a cup hook to suspend it from before you start.

If you would like to just make a fairy light garland with stars, unroll the wire completely on the floor and fold it in half, twisting it now and then along the length before sliding the paper shapes along the wire.

Materials

- 2 x 30cm white wire floristry rings
- 10m battery-operated warm white micro fairy lights
- Galvanised steel garden wire
- Floristry reel wire
- White paper star strips
- 25mm split ring
- Hot glue gun
- Ribbon or string, for hanging
- Pliers and scissors
- Wooden kebab skewer
- Pine sprigs
- Berry sprigs (real or artificial)
- White chalk paint

1. Firstly, space the two rings apart by cutting four 10cm pieces of wire and winding them around the hoops so they are braced between 2cm and 3cm apart. Position the braces equally around the diameter of the chandelier (at this point it is worth adding a quick blob of hot glue, just to stop them slipping about while you are working).

2. Set the battery pack of the lights off to one side, leaving a 45cm length free.

3. Wind the lights around the hoops every 2 to 3cm until you have worked all the way round.

4. Twist the wire around the hoop a couple of times and then start working back the other way, giving you a criss-cross pattern.

5. As you return in the opposite direction, unroll a new section of wire every 10cm or so to make one of the drops; the ones pictured vary between 30cm and 55cm in length.

6. When you have reached the length of drop you would like, fold the wire in half, taking the rest of the roll back up to the hoop. Insert a pencil into the loop at the bottom and twist it a few times to make the drop stiffer as the wire wraps around itself.

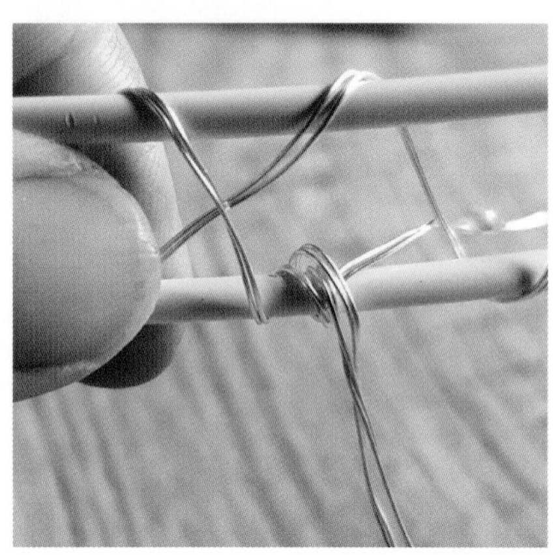

7. Taking the drop, wind it around the bottom hoop a couple of times so it stays in place and then let it hang down.

8. Continue to work around the chandelier base until you have created nine drops of varying length and arrived back at the beginning. Twiddle the end of the wire around the base to fix it in place. Do not worry if at this stage it looks quite tangled, once the lights are switched on you will only notice their glow and not the wire!

9. To make the hanger, cut two 90cm lengths of ribbon or yarn. Tie the end of one piece on to the frame, pass it through the split ring and then attach it to the opposite side. Repeat with the other length of ribbon so the chandelier hangs evenly and then hang it up, ready to attach the stars.

10. To make the paper stars, fold your strips in half lengthways if they are not already, and snip the ends off at an angle.

11. To make the first star, take four strips and alternately weave them inside and outside the adjacent strip to form a square.

12. Pull the strips so the square closes up.

13. Lay your strips out so one is pointing up at the left-hand side. Fold the top layer down.

14. Repeat with the other three strips, working anti-clockwise.

15. Take the fourth strip and tuck it into the hole made by the first strip.

16. Take the top right strip and bend it away from you, folding it into a triangle.

17. Now bend the strip towards you, up and away from you and back down through the hole by the triangle.

18. Pull the end gently until it forms a point. These are probably the hardest manoeuvres, but once you have mastered them successfully the rest of the star will be a breeze.

19. Keep turning the star 90 degrees to the right and repeating this fold until all the right-hand strips have been made into points.

20. Turn the star over and repeat until all the (new) right-hand strips have been folded. You should now have eight external points on your star.

21. Now we are going to make the internal points (the working ends of your strips should now have moved to the centre). Lift up the bottom right-hand strip.

22. Twist it down and to the right, to make a triangle.

23. Moving the working strip above it out of the way, take the end and loop it up and over, pushing it through the adjacent hole.

24. The tip should come out of the top star point to the left. Pull gently until it forms a point.

25. Repeat with the other three strips until you have four points.

26. Turn the star over and repeat with the last four strips to make four more points.

27. Snip off the excess working length where it comes through the external points. Make eighteen or so stars.

28. To fix the paper stars to the wire, take a wooden kebab stick and push it through one of the stars, in between two of the wider points; gently apply pressure until it comes through at the other side.

29. Twist the bottom of one of the wire drops into a firm point and then push it through the star, sliding it up the drop until it is in the position you would like.

30. Repeat with seventeen or eighteen more stars around the chandelier, adjusting them so they hang at different heights.

31. Add a tiny spot of hot glue to each of the joins where the wires meet the stars to secure them in place (using the end of the kebab stick to apply it can be useful so you don't end up with massive blobs of adhesive).

32. Attach one end of the reel wire to the main hoop. Lay a sprig of pine on the outside of the chandelier and wrap the wire around the stem of the sprig to hold it in place firmly. Place another sprig over the stem and continue to wrap, working all the way round until the whole base is covered. Add in a few berries as you go, if you would like a little burst of colour.

33. Snip the reel wire and wrap round the base a few times to tie it off.

34. To dust the pine with a little 'snow', water down a couple of tablespoons of white chalk paint with an equal amount of water. Dip an old toothbrush or paint brush into the mixture, shake off any excess and then gently apply to the pine sprigs. Allow to dry.

35. Suspend your chandelier from a ceiling hook, hanging the battery pack up as well and disguising it with a couple more sprigs. Surplus stars can be hung on the tree, used as table scatters, or fixed on to kebab skewers to make simple plant pot sticks.

36. The paper trimmings need not be wasted either; glue into quick and easy paper chains, or fold into little hearts to hang on the tree.

WHITE CLAY ORNAMENTS

As anyone who has ever made salt dough decorations can tell you, the joy of modelling can be outweighed by the fact that prolonged exposure to the salt can leave your hands feeling decidedly sore and itchy. This clay is a dream to use, however, as its silky smooth texture is both pliable and effortlessly imprinted. Easily stamped out with cookie cutters, all sorts of interesting textures can be created by gently pushing a variety of household items into the dough; I personally like using twigs and leaves for an organic effect, but old lace fabric, letter stamps and cookie presses can all add a lovely festive touch.

The clay can also be scented using a few drops of essential oil such as cinnamon and orange. Add this when you are kneading the dough after it has cooled down; we added an experimental glug of lavender before we heated it in the saucepan and the house smelt like a 1960s hair salon for the rest of the evening. I would also air dry the clay if you have scented it, as the scent can bake out, as it were (although you can just as easily add a couple of drops to the back of each ornament before you hang it).

GOD
JUL

Another wonderful reason for making this dough is that it can be rolled out and squidged back together multiple times, ideal if you are making this with creative yet indecisive kids. The clay also keeps beautifully for a good couple of weeks if wrapped tightly in a plastic bag, so is a great craft idea to plan for if you know there is a rainy afternoon ahead.

Ingredients

- 1 cup bicarbonate of soda
- ½ cup cornflour
- ¾ cup of warm water

1. Place all the ingredients in a medium-sized saucepan and heat gently until the mixture starts to bubble, stirring constantly with a wooden spoon.

2. As the mixture starts to thicken, continue to beat it with the spoon until it starts to come away from the edge of the pan, just as if you were making choux pastry.

3. Tip the thickened paste on to a board, liberally dusted with more cornflour, and leave to cool.

4. Once the dough has reached room temperature, knead it thoroughly until smooth; add a few drops of essential oil if you like, and dust on more cornflour if the paste is still too sticky.

5. Roll out until it is roughly 4–5mm thick (I have two chunky bamboo scent diffuser sticks I use as guides for the rolling pin, which helps keep the thickness even). If you would like to imprint any twigs or foliage, now is the time! Lay them out on the surface of the dough and then gently roll over the top with your rolling pin, pushing down gently.

6. Peel the leaves/twigs away from the clay, then stamp out your design using cookie cutters or a wine glass. I use a metal drinking straw for making the hanging holes, periodically blowing down the other end to clear any blockages.

7. Wooden letter stamps can be used to write personalised Christmas greetings, either plain or with coloured ink; I find it easier to line the letters up into a block and push them all in simultaneously rather than using the letters one by one as it is much easier to centralise them this way.

8. Lay your designs out on a baking sheet to dry.

9. The ornaments can be left to air dry, which will take 1–2 days depending on how damp the air is. They can also be dried in the oven if you need them in a hurry (although the finish may tend towards a biscuity beige, rather than a crisp white). Preheat the oven to 75°C and bake the decorations for about an hour to an hour and a half, turning them periodically, then leave to cool. They might take slightly longer, depending on the size and thickness of the ornaments, so keep an eye on them.

10. Once they are fully dried, smooth off any rough edges with a little piece of fine sandpaper or an old emery board. Extra embellishments can also be drawn or painted on at this stage; I would recommend using acrylic paint pens rather than paint, as the water content in the latter will make them sticky.

11. String on pretty ribbon or baker's twine, and hang on your tree, or use as festive personalised gift tags.

HOME
HYGGE

While the ornaments can be strung individually or horizontally to make garlands for your Christmas tree, this homely wall-hanging will add a little texture to any wall or window. It was made using white clay hearts with either one or two holes punched into the dough, and macramé cord threaded through them once they were dry. Sawing the ends off a stick that was roughly 2cm in diameter, I simply tied the cords on, interspersing them with wooden beads for a bohemian feel, and added a little blob of hot glue to fix the strings in place.

JULEHJERTER

Julehjerter are traditional Danish paper heart baskets, the oldest known example of which was made by Hans Christian Andersen, and which can still be seen in a museum in Odense, Denmark. He would spend hours cutting paper silhouettes (of which around 400 still survive), and would make and hand them out to children as he told his wonderful stories.

These ornaments are a great way to get kids involved in festive activities (and away from their phones), and all you need is paper, scissors and Sellotape or glue. Once you have mastered the art of weaving them, they can also be made with felt for a slightly more durable ornament, and the number of tabs can be increased for a more complex design; just remember that each 'finger' has to be the same length as the width of the heart. They look lovely either strung on ribbon as pretty bunting, or hung on the tree and filled with tiny sweets.

1. Cut out two pieces of different coloured paper using the template at the back of the book; red and white are the most traditional.

2. Fold each piece in half and make two equidistant cuts just up to where the edge of the heart starts to bend.

3. Weave the paper as shown; the first strip (1) will go outside C, through B and outside A. Strip 2 goes through C, over B and inside A, while strip 3 should be outside C, passing through B before ending up outside A.

4. Cut a piece of paper for the handle and glue on as shown.

WALNUT PIXIES

These dear little walnut babies are so quick to make in batches; in fact the hardest part is cracking the shells neatly. Pre-prepared walnut shells are available to purchase specifically for crafts, but the problem with that is that you don't get to eat the nut itself. The easiest way to split them in half neatly takes a little preparation but should guarantee a higher success rate than if you just attack them with a nutcracker (older walnuts will split more easily than fresh ones).

Soak the nuts overnight in a bowl of boiling water. Rinse them and dry thoroughly. Take a sharp knife and carefully push it into the split at the rounded end of the nut, then gently wiggle towards one side along the crease. Remove the knife, turn the nut round and once again wiggle down the split. Now place the knife horizontally along the split and gently push down on the knife, applying firm pressure. The walnut should open into two equal halves; it probably won't work every time, but certainly gives you a higher success rate than any other method. (The leftover walnut

pieces are delicious plunged into a jar of golden runny honey, steeped for a few days and then spooned over creamy natural yoghurt for breakfast).

Once you have cracked the trick of splitting the walnuts open, there are so many speedy ways of making dinky decorations. Sweet fairy-tale ornaments can be created by gluing toadstool picks into the base along with a smattering of reindeer moss, and the little cottages in the picture were made with a tiny lump of white clay, formed into small cubes and then pinched into a house shape.

Materials

- Walnut shells
- Cotton wool balls
- 25mm jacquard ribbon
- Knitted glove
- Baker's twine or paper ribbon
- Needle and thread
- Hot glue gun
- Fine marker pens

1. Cut a 4–5cm section of ribbon; if it has a pattern make sure it is centred where you would like. Thread the needle with a double length of cotton and then sew a line of tiny running stitches along the bottom of the ribbon.

2. Draw the thread up gently so the ribbon makes a 'cup' shape; don't pull it all the way as then you won't get such a rounded bed shape.

3. Glue half a ball of cotton wool into the base of the shell to fill it, then add another little blob of adhesive to its pointy end and attach the two ends of the twine to make a hanging loop.

4. Take the ruched ribbon and glue half a cotton wool ball to the reverse side to puff it out, then add more adhesive and secure it to the lower half of the walnut shell.

5. To make the head and hat, firstly draw a tiny face on the wooden bead, ensuring the holes are pointing vertically. I always think it is best to draw the features on at this stage then if it ends up with a face like a baby gargoyle you can always spin it round and have another go at it.

6. Snip a 4cm section of finger from the glove and roll the cut edge over twice to create a little knitted hat. Insert the glue gun and add a couple of blobs of adhesive to secure the brim, and then squirt a generous amount up inside the hat. While the glue is still warm and pliable, pinch the front and back of the hat together. Blob a little more

glue on the left-hand side of the hat at the top, then fold it over and attach it to the brim.

7. Insert the bead just under the brim, adding a blob more adhesive if necessary, and hold it in place until it sets.

8. Glue the whole hat/head combo into the walnut shell, nestling it snugly under the blanket.

UPCYCLED SOCK NISSER (GNOMES)

These festive gnomes are so quick to make and don't even require any sewing, just a hot glue and scissors. We always seem to have an excess of single socks every time I do any laundry, so it is a great way of recycling them.

When cutting the faux fur, the trick is to cut only the backing fabric and not the actual fibres themselves, otherwise you will end up with an uneven finish. The easiest way to do this using scissors is by marking out the shape you require on the backing (ensuring the fur is pointing down) and then making lots of small snips, brushing the nap away from the cut edge as you work. However, it is much quicker to use a sharp craft knife if you have one, then you can

regulate the depth of the cut and ensure you don't hack into the beard fluff itself.

Materials

- 2 socks, ideally in different colours
- 1kg of rice
- Hot glue gun
- Elastic band
- Wooden beads (12mm in this case)
- White faux fur

1. Fill one of the socks with rice to make the base of the gnome. The quickest method for this without making a dreadful mess is by filling a pint glass with rice, putting the sock over the rim and then inverting the glass. Repeat with the second pint of rice.

2. Mould the sock between your hands until you have an even, cone-shaped base then fix the elastic band around the top.

3. Snip off the excess sock fabric and then apply a ring of hot glue around the elastic band, pushing the trimmed material into the adhesive to secure it.

4. Snip your faux fabric into a beard shape, cutting out a small V-shape from the top edge. Apply a line of glue to the top at the back and then fix on to the base, about halfway up.

5. Take your second sock and pull it down over the base so the hem is covering the top of the beard, folding it up into a nice brim. Make sure the heel is pointing towards the back of the gnome.

6. Add a dab of hot glue to one of the holes on the wooden bead and then push it into the V-shaped cut to make a nose.

7. Blob a little more on the second bead hole and bring the hat down to cover it.

8. Working round the brim of the hat, add more adhesive and secure it to the body.

9. Tie a section of ribbon or baker's twine around the top of the hat, then snip off any excess.

10. To make a girl gnome, the process is the same, except for the lack of beard. Cut three thin strips of fur fabric or chunky wool, and plait them together to make a braid, tying off one end with baker's twine in a bow. Repeat to make a second braid.

11. Glue the braids underneath the hat brim before fixing on the nose.

MINI NISSER

These friendly little chaps are made in a similar way to the sock gnomes, and can be made in just minutes using odd gloves. If you intend to stand them up, use rice as the stuffing to give them a solid base upon which to stand; if hanging on the tree, cotton wool will be lighter and ensure they don't bend the branches down too much. They look adorable as an embellishment on a special gift or glued on to brooch backs.

Materials

- 2 gloves in different colours
- Rice or cotton wool
- Small elastic bands
- Baker's twine or ribbon
- Hot glue gun
- 10mm wooden beads
- Little bells
- 15mm brooch backs (optional)

1. Snip one of the fingers off a glove, and three-quarters fill with cotton wool/rice to make the base.

2. Tie with a small elastic band or some cotton thread and then add a dab of hot glue to secure it.

3. Cut a finger from your second glove for the hat, then fold the cut edge over twice to make a brim. Apply a scant line of glue under the brim to fix it in place.

4. Cut a piece from the faux fur, roughly 2cm wide and 2cm long and tapering down to a point. Glue on to the body about halfway up.

5. Glue the nose to the top edge of the beard, ensuring the lower hole is angled back in towards the beard. Snuggle the hat down over the body. Add a blob of hot glue at the back to attach it firmly

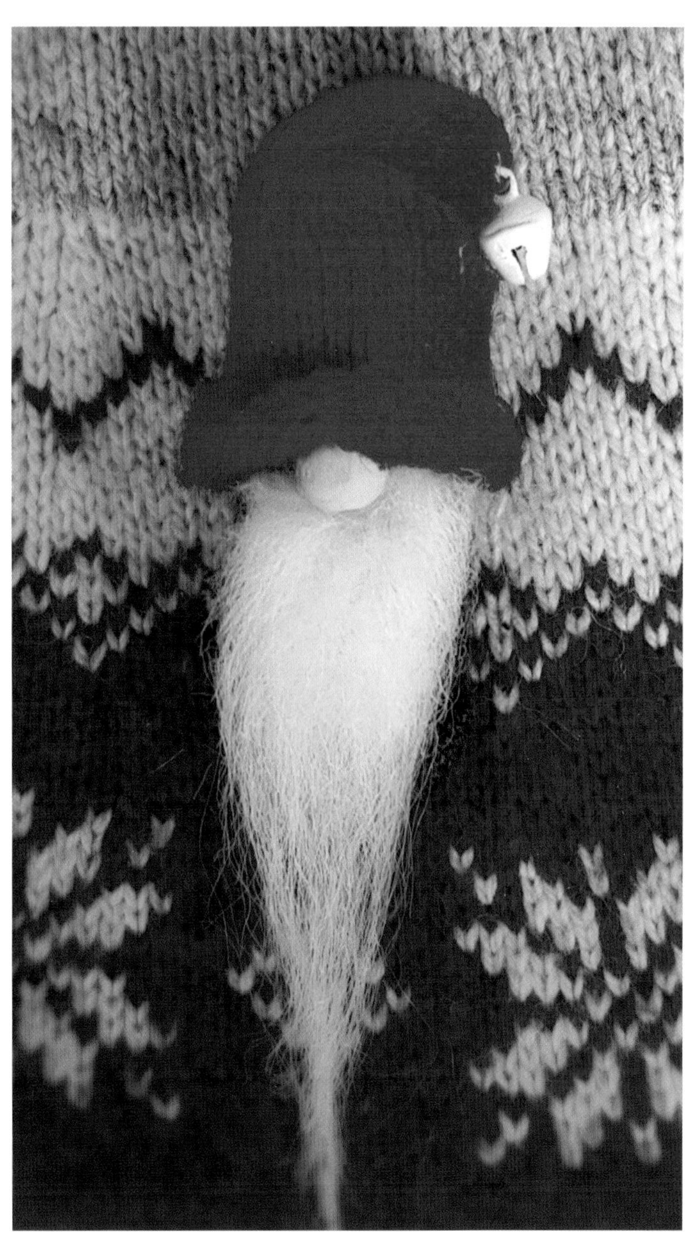

and then again on either side of the nose, pulling the hat down and pressing it down on both sides of the bead.

6. For a hanging gnome, snip the top off the hat. Add a blob of adhesive inside the finger, and attach a 10cm piece of baker's twine to form a loop. Allow to dry and then tie the top of the hat with ribbon or more twine.

7. To make a brooch, glue the tip of the hat down at an angle, then stitch on a little bell.

8. Glue or stitch the brooch pin on to the back of the gnome.

MOSSED CANDLE WREATH

I happen to be blessed with a lawn that is mostly moss; not ideal for croquet but excellent for flower arranging, thus it was the work of but moments to gather enough for this festive candle ring, lush with evergreens and studded with berries and star anise. Mossing is a great technique for making wreaths and small ornaments, as not only can it be foraged for free from the garden, it retains moisture well and is a much more sustainable option than oasis foam. Oasis foam has latterly fallen out of fashion as it does not biodegrade and just breaks down into smaller particles which enter the water system or landfill. This is therefore a much greener option; the moss can be reused for other projects if you dampen it again and the wire frame can also be recycled many times.

If you are going to collect your own moss, make sure you don't pick it all from the same place, and pick out any blades of grass or detritus before you start. It is also available to purchase from floristry supply websites (I quite often just pop into the local florist and they are always happy to give me a little bag).

Here the candle ring is made from a piece of garden wire, but once you have worked out how to pack the moss together and tie it on to a base, much larger pieces are easy to make, using either ready-made mossing rings or rolled up sections of chicken wire formed into a ring. As with the silver birch wreath, a spot of foul and blustery weather is your friend here, blowing down all sorts of interesting branches and cones. Supplement these with some dried orange slices, perhaps a few star anise or cinnamon sticks and a burst of festive colour from some berries.

Materials

- Moss (either foraged from the garden or purchased online)
- Thick garden wire
- Masking tape
- Jute string
- Floristry wire
- Evergreen sprigs
- Berry sprays
- Star anise
- An orange
- Ribbon
- Hot glue gun
- Pillar candle

1. To dry the orange slices, preheat the oven to a low temperature of about 100°C, then cut the oranges into slices roughly 0.75mm thick. Pat them dry with kitchen paper and place on a wire rack over a baking tray, before popping them in the oven for 2–3 hours until they are dry. Turn them occasionally as they can scorch quite easily, and remove any thinner slices once they are done (they are delicious when dipped in dark chocolate).

2. If the moss is very dry, soak it in a little water and then squeeze out any excess moisture.

3. To make the moss base, form your piece of wire into a circle that will slip over the candle with plenty of room to spare; my candle was 8cm in diameter so the wire ring measured 16cm. Tape over the join with a little strip of masking tape to fix it in place and protect your fingers.

4. Tie the jute string on to the wire ring, and then taking a handful of moss, form it around the wire into a sausage shape. Wrap the string around the bundle tightly, then keep moving around the wreath, binding on more handfuls of moss as you go.

5. Once the ring has been fully covered, go round for a second time, laying on the evergreen sprigs, binding them on and then adding more over the top of the stems.

6. Tie off the string.

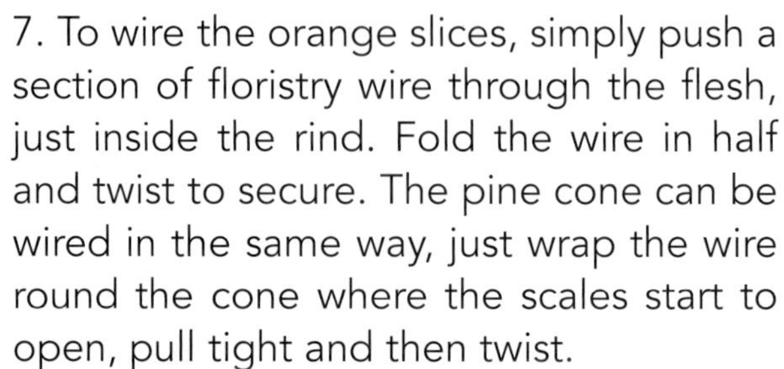

7. To wire the orange slices, simply push a section of floristry wire through the flesh, just inside the rind. Fold the wire in half and twist to secure. The pine cone can be wired in the same way, just wrap the wire round the cone where the scales start to open, pull tight and then twist.

8. Lay the candle wreath on a large plate and place the pillar candle in the centre. Tuck in some moss to fill any gaps, and then attach the orange slices and pine cones by pushing their wires into the greenery.

9. Lastly, attach the star anise and cinnamon sticks, blobbing a little dot of hot glue on and pressing firmly on to the wreath.

10. Add a little water to the plate occasionally, to keep the moss damp and prolong the life of the greenery, avoiding the orange slices.

NORDIC WINTER VILLAGE

Think of iconic Scandinavian buildings and you will no doubt recall that deep glorious rust red, seen everywhere from Danish townhouses to Swedish barns and summerhouses. This tradition dates back centuries; historically the softwoods used for building would need protection from the elements, so were painted with a mixture of linseed oil, starch (often rye flour) and iron oxide, giving that beautiful deep red. In Denmark, ochre was also used, resulting in a fabulous mustard shade; richer folk could afford colours based on more expensive pigments (such as grey), which were used to imitate stone.

There is something about sitting and painting little wooden houses that brings

me unutterable joy for some reason, as I imagine all the tiny people who live there skiing home after a hard day's work lost in a miniature blizzard. We have an Elf Village that we display from the beginning of December, and although it started as just a small settlement on a piece of driftwood, it now takes up four bookshelves and a coffee table, such is the expansionist building programme of the elves.

You have lots of options for this particular project; I collected the wood for the houses and the base from a windswept local beach, but log slices (available to purchase from craft shops) also make an attractive base. If you don't fancy sawing the buildings yourself, they can also be bought ready-made from good craft shops, or are easily shaped from air drying clay.

Materials

- Wooden houses (these measured 5cms high, 2cms deep)
- Twigs (silver birch left over from the wreath project is ideal)
- Driftwood/wooden base
- Reindeer moss or lichen
- White PVA glue
- White chalk paint
- Coloured acrylic paints
- Paint pens
- 25mm and 65mm nails
- Hammer
- Ribbon
- Drill
- Scissors
- Floristry reel wire
- Wooden drink stirrers

1. Cut your little houses to shape and paint with chalk paint, adding blobs of coloured acrylic to the paint to achieve the colours you desire.

2. Brush the roofs with a smattering of white chalk paint to give the impression of snow.

3. Paint on the windows and doors by drawing squares of white paint on to the buildings, and then detailing in black planes of glass with a paint pen. I also drew a few hearts here and there, some tiny wreaths of greenery on the front door, and a little candle arch in one of the windows.

4. Add chimneys by drilling a small hole in the roof and then gently tapping in a 25mm nail (as the houses are quite small they can split if you try and bang a nail in directly).

6

8

9

12

5. To make the flag, cut a 2cm scrap of ribbon then coat it in a very thin layer of white glue. Fold around the top of a 65mm nail and snip into shape once dry.

6. Snip six or so 2cm sections of twig and glue together to make a wood pile. The little sledge is made by cutting a 1cm section of the wooden drink stirrer to make the seat. Split a 2cm piece in half lengthways, then glue underneath to make the runners.

7. Assemble the village by gluing the houses on to the base.

8. Add the trees by drilling into the base, blobbing some glue on to the bottom of the twigs and then inserting them into the holes; you may need to trim the twigs with a craft knife to ensure a snug fit.

9. Make the fence by tapping a few small nails into the base and then winding round a length of reel wire.

10. Drill a hole for the flag post and glue the nail in position.

11. Tiny birds can be cut from empty mince pie tins, snipped into shape with scissors and painted with chalk paint. Fix in place with a small dot of glue.

12. Liberally apply some PVA to a few pieces of reindeer moss or lichen foraged from the forest floor, and then attach to the base to make the bushes and greenery.

13. Using a brush, apply a liberal coat of white chalk paint to the trees, roofs, moss and base for a snowy effect. As it dries it will contract, giving a lovely texture to the snow.

CHAPTER TWO

EDIBLE GIFTS

CHOCOLATE SALAMI

We all know that home-made gifts are special at this time of year, but making truffles can be time consuming, and the biscuits you are trying to knock up for your sister-in-law never seem to look quite as good as the ones in the recipe book ... so fear no more, as I have a fabulous, easy, no-fail gift recipe right here.

Chocolate salami is not as strange as it sounds. A traditional sweet on the continent, it is a roll of rich dark chocolate, packed with nuts and fruit, and is perfect when served with an after-dinner coffee. Packaged in baking parchment and tied with pretty ribbon, it will make a lovely little hostess gift or stocking filler; even more wonderfully, it will last for two weeks in the fridge or two months in the freezer so you can prepare ahead.

Once you have acquired the ratio of chocolate to biscuit, it is easy to create different versions as the mix is so versatile; add a pinch of salt and chilli for a more grown-up taste or perhaps use mixed dried fruit and half a teaspoon of mixed spice for a Christmas pudding flavour.

Ingredients (makes 2 x 20cm chocolate salami)

- 200g dark chocolate
- 125g butter
- 100g of biscuits. I used rich tea, but ginger nuts would be lovely for a spicier version.
- 100g glacé cherries
- 100g walnuts
- 2tbsp of liqueur (optional). I like to add a dash of either dark rum or Disaronno, but if there are kids involved, please feel free to leave this out.

1. Place the biscuits in a ziplock bag and give them a rough pounding with a rolling pin. Some dust is fine, but make sure you leave most of them in quite chunky pieces, to add texture to the salami.

2. Roughly chop the glacé cherries and walnuts, again leaving some bigger chunks.

3. Melt the chocolate and butter in a bain-marie or microwave, stirring frequently until luscious and smooth. Remove from the heat.

4. Tip the other ingredients into the chocolate mix. Stir to combine, then cover and pop in the fridge for an hour.

5. Cut two or three 20cm long pieces of cling film and overlap lengthways on your work surface to make one slightly thicker layer.

6. Spoon out half the mix on to the cling film in a rough sausage shape. Roll up tightly and twist both ends, then roll the sausage backwards and forwards to make it smooth and regular in appearance.

7. Repeat with the other half of the mix, then place the sausages in the fridge overnight to set (although in practice you can probably get away with just a couple of hours if you are desperate).

8. Unwrap the salamis and rub icing sugar all over them to give a dusted appearance, then re-wrap in squares of baking parchment and tie with ribbon.

9. Slice into sections and serve with coffee or as an after-dinner treat. (If you are going to freeze them, just unwrap the cling film, dust in sugar and roll them up in tinfoil.)

MARZIPAN

Once you have made your own marzipan, you will never go back to shop-bought. Lighter in texture and appearance than the mass-produced version, it will keep for a week in the fridge, wrapped in cling film. If you are using it for your Christmas cake, let it dry for at least twenty-four hours before you cover it in fondant/royal icing; allowing the excess moisture to evaporate will ensure that it remains edible for 1–2 months.

The recipe below should be enough to ice one 20cm Christmas cake, but it is delicious stuffed into dates, as a lining for mince pies, dotted through a boozy bread and butter pudding, and even scattered through apple crumble topping.

Ingredients

- 250g ground almonds
- 150g caster sugar
- 150g icing sugar, sifted
- 1 egg
- 1tsp almond essence
- 1tbsp brandy, optional

1. Sieve the icing sugar into a large bowl, then stir in the caster sugar and almonds.

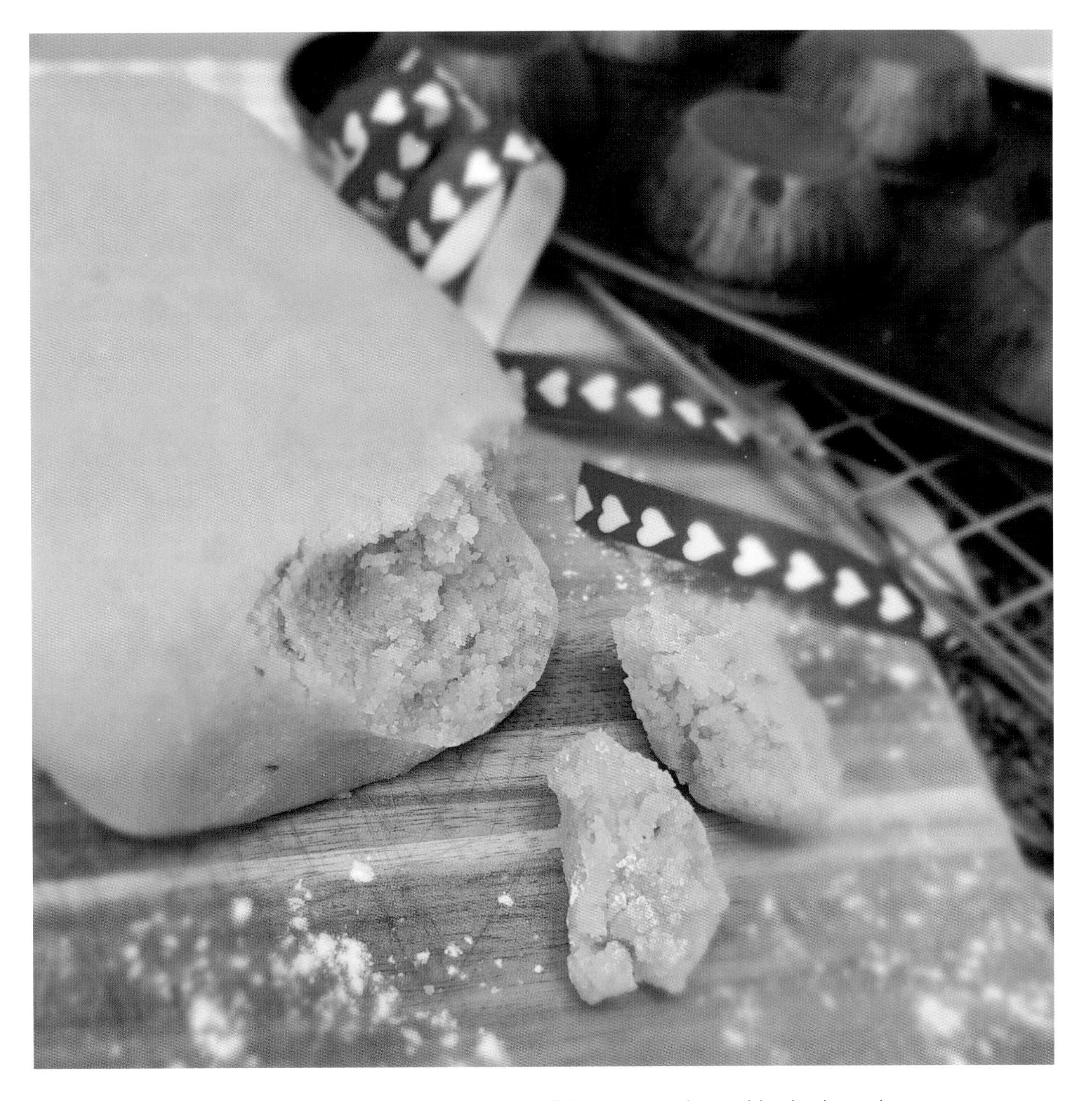

2. Crack the egg into the centre of the mix, and sprinkle the brandy and almond essence over.

3. Using a palette knife, stir to combine then turn out on to a board dusted with icing sugar.

4. Knead into a smooth paste (taking care not to over-knead, as over-handling may cause excess oil to seep out of the ground almonds and make the marzipan greasy).

5. Pop it in the freezer if you are prepping ahead of time for an organised Christmas.

MARZIPAN CHOCOLATES

These sumptuous little treats are the perfect after-dinner sweetie – rich and dark with a hint of rum. They are also a great way of using up any marzipan trimmings left after you have iced your Christmas cake.

Not normally one for making things evenly sized, I used scales to ensure that all the sweets were the same dimensions, and delegated the task of weighing the marzipan and rolling it into balls to my son and nephew. We found 11g pieces to be just right for popping whole in one's mouth.

Ingredients

- 300g marzipan
- 2tbsp rum
- 75g chopped walnuts
- 200g dark chocolate
- Icing sugar

1. Mix the marzipan, rum and walnuts together in a bowl and then roll into small balls; if you find the mixture becomes too sticky, just knead through a little icing sugar to firm it up.

2. Melt the chocolate slowly in a bain-marie, and stir until smooth.

3. Dip the marzipan balls in the chocolate, using two forks to pick them up and place on a wire rack until nearly set.

4. As soon as they are firm (but not hard) remove them with a palette knife and leave on a sheet of greaseproof paper until properly set. (If you leave them on the wire rack too long they will get stuck, says the voice of experience; likewise if you leave them to set straight on the paper they will end up sitting in puddles of chocolate.)

5. Place in petit four cases and store in an airtight tin until needed.

BRÆNDTE MANDLER (SUGAR ROASTED ALMONDS)

Carts selling hot sugared almonds are a common sight at most European Christmas markets. Powdery sugar, crispy almonds and a hint of cinnamon all combine to create a wonderfully festive

combination, and they make a great little table gift or stocking filler. Stored in glass jars they should theoretically last for a couple of weeks, but I like to pack them into tiny paper cones; stuffed in your pocket they make a delicious snack on any winter walk.

Ingredients (makes twelve small cones, plus extra for sampling)

- 200g white granulated sugar
- 200g whole almonds
- 80ml water
- ½tsp cinnamon

1. Place the water, cinnamon and sugar in a large heavy-based saucepan or frying pan, and bring to the boil over a medium-high heat, stirring constantly with a wooden spoon.

2. Once the sugar has dissolved, tip in the almonds and simmer for about ten minutes, stirring frequently.

3. The mixture will bubble away until the water has evaporated; as soon as the sugar starts to recrystallise, turn the heat down and keep turning the almonds until they are all coated in the golden crusty sugar and spice.

4. If you prefer your almonds to be smoother and glossier, just keep stirring a little longer; the sugar will start to melt again and make a shiny, caramel finish.

5. Tip the almonds out on to a sheet of baking parchment, and using two forks, separate the nuts so they do not stick together as they harden.

6. To make the paper cones, cut twelve circles from a roll of baking parchment, using a dinner plate as a template (the one used here was 27cm in diameter).

7. Fold the paper circle in half, shiny side facing inwards, then in half twice more to make the cone shape.

8. Fill with between twelve and fourteen almonds, then tie with baker's twine in a pretty bow.

ROMKUGLER (RUM BALLS)

This is probably the least realistic project in the book, in that it assumes you will have leftover cake in the house. Romkugler were traditionally made by Danish bakers as a way of using up leftover pastries and cakes at the end of the day. Not a problem I suffer from, to be honest, but if you are prepared to squirrel away the odd muffin or pain au chocolat, pop them in the freezer until you have enough for the recipe. I, on the other hand, have to go and buy

cake for the purpose, but I find supermarket 'cheap and cheerful' Madeira sponge an excellent way of coping with the problem.

These delicious treats are perfect to make with children, as they can take over the task of rolling the balls while you enjoy a cup of tea and supervise from a comfy chair. I love them made with spiced rum, but if you prefer to make them without alcohol, either vanilla or rum essence will both work nicely (add a couple of tablespoons of orange juice to make up the amount of liquid). A kitchen mixer or food processor will make life much easier as well, although they can be made (fairly laboriously) by just mashing up everything with a fork.

Ingredients (makes 30–40)

- 500g leftover cake or Danish pastry
- 100g marzipan
- 3tbsp raspberry jam
- 3tbsp cocoa powder, plus extra for dusting
- 2tbsp rum
- 150g chocolate vermicelli

1. Grate the marzipan (this is made easier if you put it in the fridge for half an hour first).

2. Place the marzipan, cake, jam and cocoa powder either into a food processor or a stand mixer with the beater attachment.

3. Mix/whizz until the mixture becomes a smooth paste; to start with, you will think 'oh, that's never going to work', then all of a sudden the ingredients will change from a crumby mess to a glorious chocolate squidge.

4. Now is the ideal moment to scoop out a sample and invite family members to air their opinion regarding the blend of flavours, and add more cocoa or marzipan accordingly. (I always plump for the 'it needs more rum' option.)

5. Once everyone is happy, pop the mix in the fridge for half an hour to let it firm up a little.

6. Form into balls (about 15g or the size of a small walnut) then roll them in either chocolate vermicelli or sieved cocoa for a richer, more adult palate.

7. Place in petit four cases and serve. The romkugler will last about a week in an airtight tin, but can be made ahead of time and stored in the freezer for a month if you have used fresh cake/pastry.

HOKEY-POKEY

Hokey-pokey, also known as cinder toffee or honeycomb, is a crunchy symphony of bubbles and pure sugar, and as such is beloved of all children. I had tried making honeycomb a couple of times in the past and on both occasions it resulted in a sticky kitchen and the throwing-away of a hitherto perfectly acceptable saucepan. However, the use of a thermometer has transformed the cooking process and now it never fails; I use slightly less bicarbonate of soda

than other recipes as I find higher quantities can result in a slightly soapy flavour. It is also a good idea to pre-fill your washing up bowl with very hot water to put your saucepan in immediately you have tipped the mixture out, as it makes cleaning up a breeze.

This is another great recipe to make with kids as the way the mixture foams up like a small volcano can be rather exciting and the basis of an impromptu science lesson; when the bicarbonate of soda is added to the sugar syrup it causes the release of carbon dioxide. This is trapped as bubbles in the cooling sugar, thus giving the honeycomb texture. However, the molten syrup will be terrifyingly hot so please make sure children stay at a safe distance throughout the whole cooking process.

Store in an airtight glass jar for up to a month, and place in little bags when you are ready to give it away; the crumbs left over when the honeycomb is smashed up can be stored separately and give a lovely sweet crunch to an otherwise unexciting ice cream.

Ingredients

- 200g caster sugar
- 100g golden syrup
- 1½tsp bicarbonate of soda (if yours has been sitting in the cupboard for two years it might be worth getting a new tub as it can affect how the mixture foams up).

1. Line a roasting tin with greaseproof paper.

2. Find the largest saucepan you have, and slowly heat the caster sugar and syrup over a medium heat until the sugar has dissolved.

3. Bring to the boil then turn the heat down and simmer until the mixture has just started to turn a lovely amber colour and your thermometer reads 150°C.

4. Now take the saucepan off the heat and quickly stir in the bicarbonate of soda. When it starts to foam up, tip it into the roasting tin; once you've poured it out it is very important to not touch it or the bubbles will collapse.

5. Leave for a good hour or so until it has gone completely cold then break into chunks. Larger pieces can be dipped in melted chocolate and left to cool on greaseproof paper, to make extra special little treats for a winter walk or film night.

FUDGY BROWNIES JAR

Batch-making Christmas gifts has never been easier than with these easy chocolate brownie jars. More of a production line than a recipe, the dry ingredients are layered in 1 litre glass containers ready for the recipient to just add eggs and melted butter. The result is a gloriously gooey and rich confection, punctuated with dark chocolate chunks and crunchy almonds for the perfect afternoon

snack; they taste even better on the second day, if they last that long. There is also plenty of room left in the jar if you wish to add a handful of dried cranberries or raisins.

Ingredients (to fill a 1 litre jar)

- 200g dark chocolate, chopped
- 150g caster sugar
- 150g demerara sugar
- 75g plain flour
- 40g cocoa powder
- 25g flaked almonds

1. Roughly chop the chocolate and set aside.

2. Add the ingredients to the jar as follows, spooning them in carefully and occasionally shaking the container gently to even out the layers: flour, cocoa, white sugar, golden sugar, almonds and chocolate chunks.

3. I find it useful to keep a clean tea towel close to hand so you can wipe the inside of the jar in between layers; the cocoa in particular likes to stick to the glass. If you fancy changing the ingredients, such as using milk chocolate chips or walnuts for example, always place the largest ingredients on top, as the finer ones will filter down.

4. Pack any remaining space left in the top of the jar with some scrunched-up baking paper, just to stop anything moving around too much.

5. Label the jar with the following cooking instructions. 'Preheat the oven to 180°C and line a 20.5cm square tin. Melt 125g butter, stir in 3 beaten eggs and add the contents of the brownie jar. Stir well and then bake for 18–20 minutes until dry on top but still squidgy inside! Allow to cool for at least three hours before slicing.'

BRUNKAGER (BROWN COOKIES)

There are a number of reasons why I love making these Christmas biscuits, not least of all their rich and almost caramelly flavour, warmed by festive spices. It is customary in Denmark to offer hospitality to guests in the form of a drink and at least three kinds of snack. Brought up on this tradition by family, I still feel slightly offended if any visitor to my home turns down the offer of a cup of coffee and a little something, and spend the next forty minutes wondering what I have done to upset them.

The dough is made the day before you need it, in order to allow the flavours to soften and mingle, so there is very little washing up on the actual day of baking (perfect if you are expecting guests), and it can also be frozen up to a month in advance. Try and slice the dough as finely as you can, so the biscuits have a pleasing and crispy snap when broken, rather than the texture and appearance of a hobbit's roof tile.

Ingredients

- 250g plain flour
- 125g butter
- 125g soft, dark brown sugar
- 125g golden syrup
- Grated zest of one lemon
- 1 level tsp baking powder
- 2tsp cinnamon
- 1½tsp ground ginger
- ½tsp ground cloves
- ½tsp ground cardamom
- 25g flaked almonds

1. Place the butter, sugar and syrup in a saucepan and gently stir over a medium heat until everything has melted and formed a rich dark treacly goo.

2. Remove from the heat and allow to cool.

3. Sift the flour and baking powder into a large mixing bowl, then add the lemon zest, ginger, cinnamon, cardamom and cloves.

4. Pour in the melted mixture and stir the dough to combine. Add a little more flour, a spoonful at a time, if you find the dough is too sticky.

5. Turn out the mixture on to a floured board and knead gently until smooth.

6. Lay a 40cm piece of baking parchment on to a baking sheet, and gently form your dough into a sausage on top. Wrap it up in the baking parchment and roll it backwards and forwards to even out the shape. It should measure roughly 30cm by 4cm.

7. Pop the sausage in the fridge for an hour, then take it out and give it another rolling; the dough will have stiffened up by now making it easier to get a nice sausage shape.

8. Leave in the fridge overnight, then when you are ready to bake, preheat the oven to 180°C

9. Remove the dough from the fridge and cut into 4mm slices. Arrange the biscuits on lined baking sheets about 3cm apart, and then gently press a flaked almond into the centre of each one.

10. Bake in the centre of the oven for 6–8 minutes; they will crisp up as they cool.

CHRISTMAS TEA WITH ORANGE PEEL HEARTS

Studies show that cinnamon, ginger and cloves all have antioxidant and antibacterial properties so I often wonder whether this might be a reason we crave the heat of spices in the depths of winter, in order to boost our flagging immune systems. This delicious tea makes a warming drink on a cold day, with the festive fragrance of Christmas spice blending with the zest of orange. Pack into small Kilner jars along with some little muslin drawstring teabags as a welcome stocking filler; if you cannot find muslin teabags but have some of the fabric, cut some 10cm squares and put two teaspoons of the tea in the centre, before drawing up and tying with baker's twine, like a bouquet garni. Leave ample room for the tea leaves to circulate.

Ingredients

- 125g loose leaf black tea (I use Darjeeling)
- 1 orange
- 1 lemon
- 15 cloves
- 4 cardamom pods
- 3 cinnamon sticks
- 500ml Kilner jar
- Small heart cutter
- Ribbon

1. Preheat the oven to 100°C.

2. Peel strips of skin from the lemon, ensuring there is no white bitter pith remaining, and spread out on a baking sheet.

3. Cut a slice from the end of the orange and set aside.

4. Quarter the rest of the orange and scoop out the flesh with a spoon. Using a sharp knife, scrape the pith away from the skin.

5. Using the heart cutter, stamp out as many shapes as you can from the orange skin; I find it easiest to push the cutter down using a rolling pin, then it won't hurt your fingers and you can apply more force.

6. Lay the hearts out on the baking sheet with the lemon peel and orange slice, and place in the oven to dry. This should take about an hour for the little hearts and the peel, so remove these then pop the orange slice back in for another 1–2 hours, turning it periodically.

7. Put the cloves, cinnamon and cardamom pods in a mortar and roughly crush them with a pestle (if you do not have a mortar and

pestle, putting all the spices in a plastic bag and giving them a committed bash with the blunt end of a rolling pin will also work nicely).

8. Mix the spices, tea and dried citrus fruit in a small Kilner jar, tying the orange slice on to the outside with some pretty ribbon. Leave for at least a week so the flavours have time to mingle.

9. To serve the tea, add two teaspoons of the mix to your muslin tea bag, pour over hot water and steep for two minutes. Sweeten with a teaspoon of honey if you like!

APPLE CHUTNEY

My maternal grandparents were married on the eve of the Second World War, and their canny ability to make do and mend as a result of post-war thrift taught me much (although nowadays it is more fashionably known as 'crafting' and 'upcycling'). Thanks to his enviable talent for making tasty relish out of pretty much anything that grew in the garden, my grandfather was informally known as The Chutney King. This is their famous apple chutney recipe, carefully written out by my granny on the back of a recycled envelope. I have very fond memories of them standing by the stove, stirring away and chatting about batch consistency, and even now every year we still have Chutney Making Evening in their honour. This is usually

the night after a particularly blustery storm, where all the windfalls in the orchard have come down but have yet to be attacked by chickens.

The chutney tastes best after being stored for 2–3 months in a dark cupboard, so if made with autumn windfalls it will be ready just in time for your Christmas cheese and biscuits. If you have been carefully saving your jam jars all year ready for this moment, you might find that they still carry the odour of their original occupant. This is easily solved using good old bicarbonate of soda: make a paste of 3 parts soda to 1 part water, and smear over the jar and the lid. Leave overnight and rinse, and the smell of continental pickled gherkins will have vanished. Bicarbonate of soda can also be used to remove any persistent labels too. Mix with a little vegetable oil and smear over the label, before leaving for twenty-four hours. Give the tenacious sticker a vigorous scrub with a washing up cloth and it should come right off.

Use the last few spoonfuls to fill a few tiny jars as well, to pop in Christmas stockings or crackers.

Ingredients (makes about 8 x 250ml jars)

- 2kg apples, peeled, cored and chopped
- 500g onions, chopped
- 500g sultanas
- 500g soft brown sugar
- 500ml malt vinegar
- 1 crushed clove of garlic
- 1tsp ground ginger
- 1tsp Maldon salt
- ½tsp ground black peppercorns

1. Place all the ingredients in a large stainless steel preserving pan or cooking pot.

2. Bring to the boil and simmer gently, uncovered, for two and a half to three hours, stirring occasionally with a wooden spoon to prevent the chutney catching on the base of the pan.

3. Cook until reduced in volume and rich, thick and a deep caramel brown. You can tell if it is ready by drawing your wooden spoon across the bottom of the pan; there should be very little liquid to fill the gap, and it should seep back in slowly.

4. Pot while hot! Start preparing your jars when you have about

twenty minutes of cooking time left. Wash the jars and lids in hot soapy water, rinse, and then place them upside down on a baking tray and pop into an oven which has been preheated to 160–180°C. Bake for fifteen minutes before potting up.

5. I find it easiest to use a small jug to pour in the chutney as it is quite sticky and once it has been spilt down the outside of the jar it can be a nightmare to remove. Take care as the sugar content will ensure it stays hot for a while, so use a tea towel to hold the jar while you fill it, leaving about a centimetre of space at the top.

6. Cover with a waxed paper disc, screw on the lid and label when cool. It will easily last for up to a year in a dark cupboard; once opened, store in the fridge and consume within four weeks.

FRUIT VINEGAR

The one thing I am successful at growing is blackcurrants, mainly as they thrive on being left to their own devices, so every year we make a big batch of fruit vinegar to see us through the winter. Many recipes seem to call for a huge amount of sugar, but as we predominantly use it for dressings and marinades, I cut the amount of sugar down to give a tarter, less syrupy liquid; it also makes a surprisingly tasty cordial when mixed with water.

Either white wine or cider vinegar can be used, and light brown sugar will give a more caramelly flavour; this recipe works well with all sorts of soft fruits, from strawberries to blackberries.

Ingredients

- 1kg berries, fresh or frozen
- 600ml of white wine or cider vinegar
- Granulated sugar (the amount will vary according to how much juice is yielded)

1. Wash the fruit and pick out any obvious stalks or leaves, then place in a ceramic bowl. Pour over the vinegar, cover and leave to macerate for 4–5 days, periodically giving everything a bit of a squidge with a potato masher to help break up the fruit.

2. Strain into a large measuring jug through a scalded muslin, or, in this instance, a sieve lined with a sheet of kitchen paper; try not squish the fruit too much or you will end up with a cloudy vinegar.

3. Pour the juice into a non-reactive saucepan, and add 175g sugar for every 500ml of liquid.

4. Place over a medium heat and stir with a wooden spoon until the sugar has dissolved, then simmer for around ten minutes.

5. Allow to cool slightly, then pour into warm, sterilised glass bottles or jars.

COFFEE LIQUEUR

There are few things more pleasurable than a liqueur after a long family meal, and this coffee infused spirit is perfect for either serving to your guests after a dinner party, or as a little extra pick-me-up in a Christmas hamper. Quick to put together, it only takes a few key ingredients and a month-long rest in a dark cupboard before you have a silky smooth treat to serve over ice. Drizzle over vanilla ice cream with a few chopped walnuts as a quick grown-up dessert, add a glug to coffee cake mixture and truffles, or pour a dash in your hot chocolate for a treat. It also tastes delicious in a glass of ice cold milk, or as a basis for some adventurous holiday cocktails. (I confess, however, that I do use decaffeinated coffee, as I like to be able to go to bed after drinking it and still sleep.)

Ingredients (makes roughly 1.5l, allowing a little extra for tasting as you go)

- 750ml vodka
- 750ml water
- 400g brown sugar
- 50g strong instant coffee powder
- 1tbsp good quality vanilla extract

1. Place the water and sugar in a large saucepan.

2. Simmer for 5–10 minutes over medium to high heat until all the sugar has dissolved, making a syrup.

3. Add the vanilla extract and coffee and give the mixture a quick whisk until all the powder has dissolved.

4. Remove from the heat and allow to cool completely before stirring in the vodka (this last part is important as you don't want any of the alcohol to evaporate).

5. Pour into sterilised jars or bottles then leave for at least a month to allow the flavours to mellow. At this point it is worth giving it a little taste and deciding if you would like to make it any sweeter. Add caster sugar in 50g increments, shaking thoroughly and leaving it for a couple of days in between additions.

6. Strain through a coffee filter or muslin to get rid of any cloudiness or fine grounds from the coffee powder, then decant into pretty sterilised glass bottles and label ready to give as gifts.

7. Once you are happy with the recipe in terms of sugar content, it is a great one to play with; add 50g of cocoa to the initial mix to make a mocha liqueur, or swap some of the vodka for spiced rum or brandy for more complex flavours.

Coffee
Liqeur

CHAPTER THREE

QUICK AND EASY CRAFTS

COSY CROCHET INFINITY SCARF

With just one type of crochet stitch involved, this gorgeous chunky scarf can be knocked up in just an evening, and won't reduce you to a nervous wreck if you are new to the craft. It can often seem

a complicated skill to learn, especially as there are differences between the terminology used in US and UK patterns; here we are using a simple double crochet stitch (known as a single crochet in the US).

The fabulous thing about this pattern is that you don't even need a crochet hook, just your fingers. Arm knitting is very popular at the moment as a quick and easy way of creating jumbo scarves and blankets, but I find finger crochet much easier. Not only is an XL chunky wool used, so that the project grows quickly, you can also put it down whenever you fancy a cup of tea, rather than having to wait to the end of a row to disentangle yourself. The instructions are for right-handed working, so please just reverse the positions if it is easier; as each person's fingers are different sizes your tension may also vary.

The pattern below can be finished in one of two ways; either as an infinity loop or as a traditional scarf (in which case the ends look lovely with some tassels added, or gathered up and finished with a couple of fluffy pom-poms; you will require an extra ball of yarn for these options).

Materials

- 2 x 50g balls of Super Chunky (size 6) yarn (80m per ball)
- Darning needle

1. Make a slip knot at the end of your yarn by holding the working wool in your left hand and forming a loop, crossing the yarn over the top and ensuring you have a long tail of about 30cm.

2. Take the tail in your right hand and form another loop. Push this through the first loop from back to front.

3. Insert the forefinger of your right hand through the loop and pull gently on the working yarn in your left hand to form the first slip knot.

4. Wrap the working wool around your little finger, behind your second, third and fourth fingers and over the top of your left index finger.

5. Now push your thumb through the loop as well, grasp the working yarn and draw it back through the stitch, slipping the new loop on your finger. This makes your first chain stitch (the finger loop never counts as a stitch). Keep your work nice and loose.

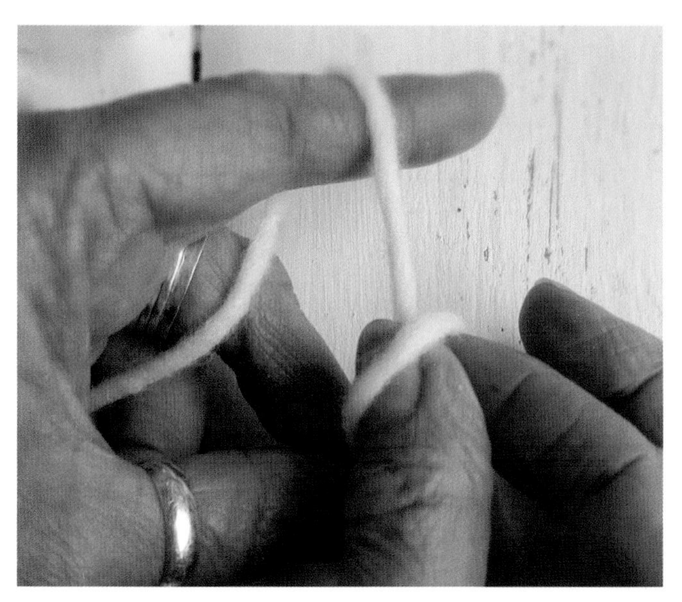

6. Continue to repeat stage 5 until your chain reaches 160cm long.

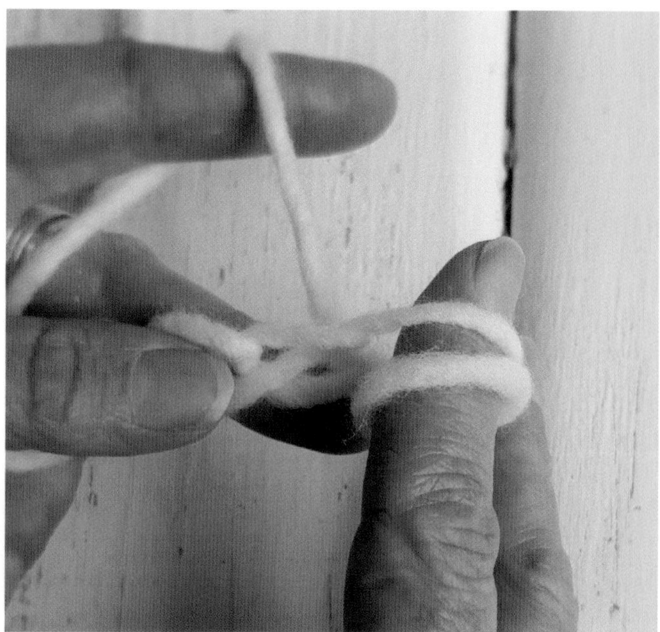

7. Once you have chained to the desired length, begin the first row. Ignoring the very first stitch, put your index finger through the second, as indicated.

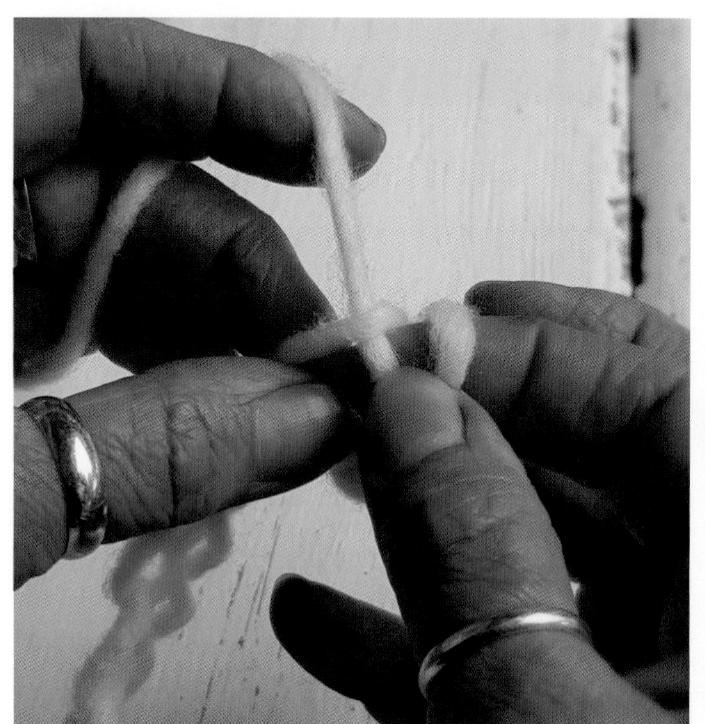

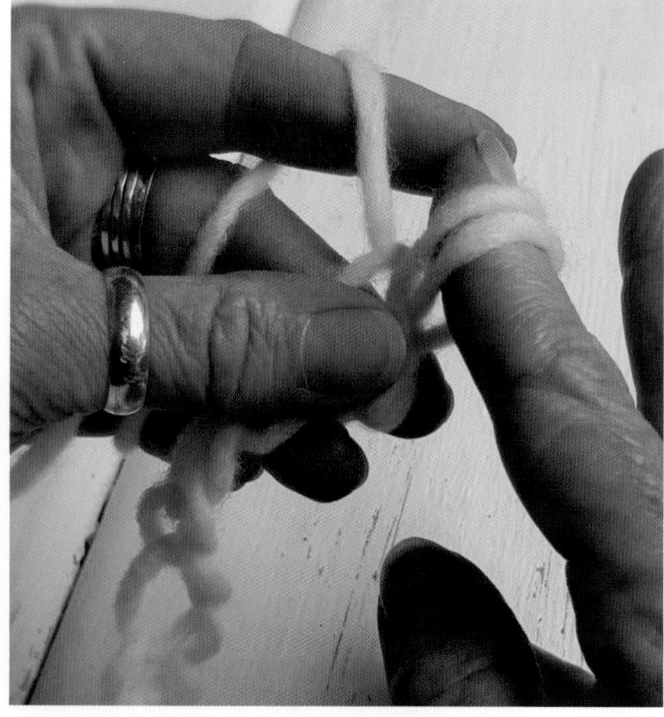

8. Hook the working yarn with your index finger (this is known as yarn over) and bring it through so you now have two loops.

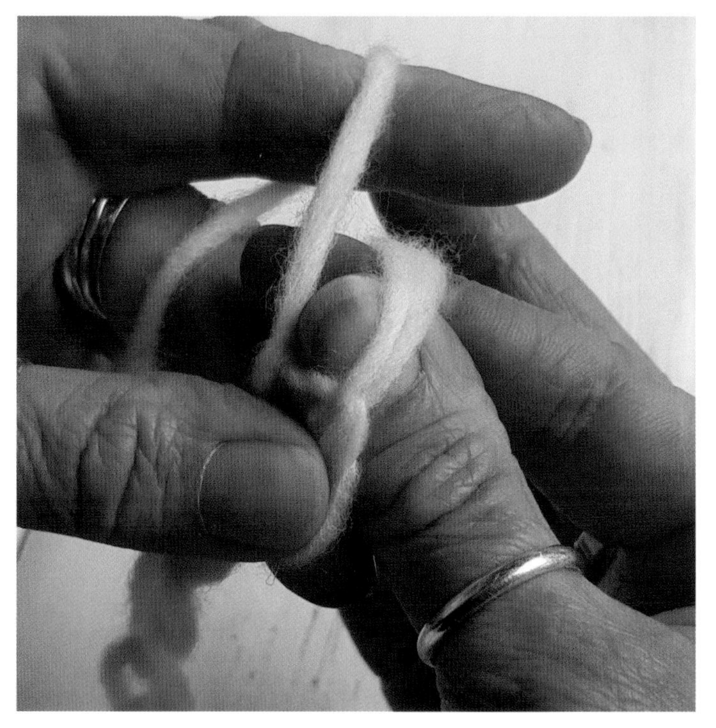

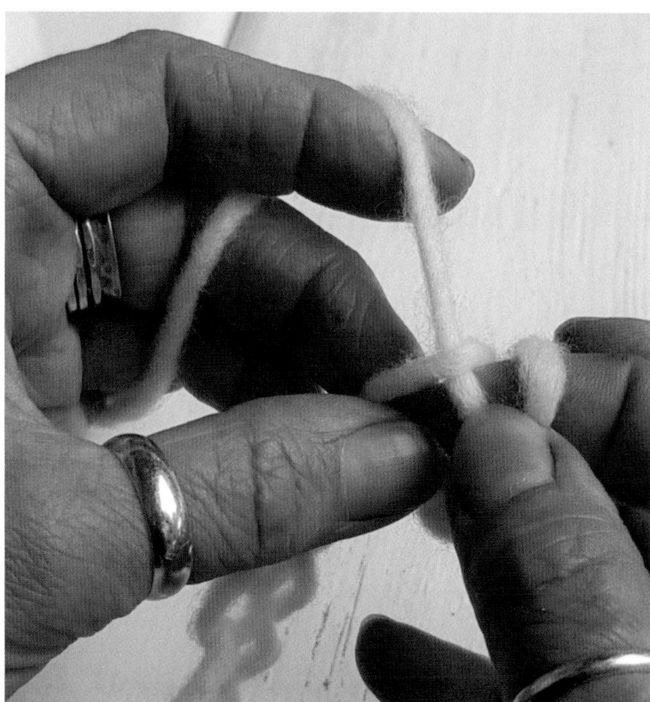

9. Push your thumb through both these loops, pinch the working yarn and draw it all the way through, slipping it back on to your index finger to make your first double crochet.

10. Repeat to the end of the chain (making sure you don't miss the very last loop as sometimes this can pull quite tight).

11. At the end of the row make an extra chain stitch (known as a turning chain) and turn the work so it is to your left.

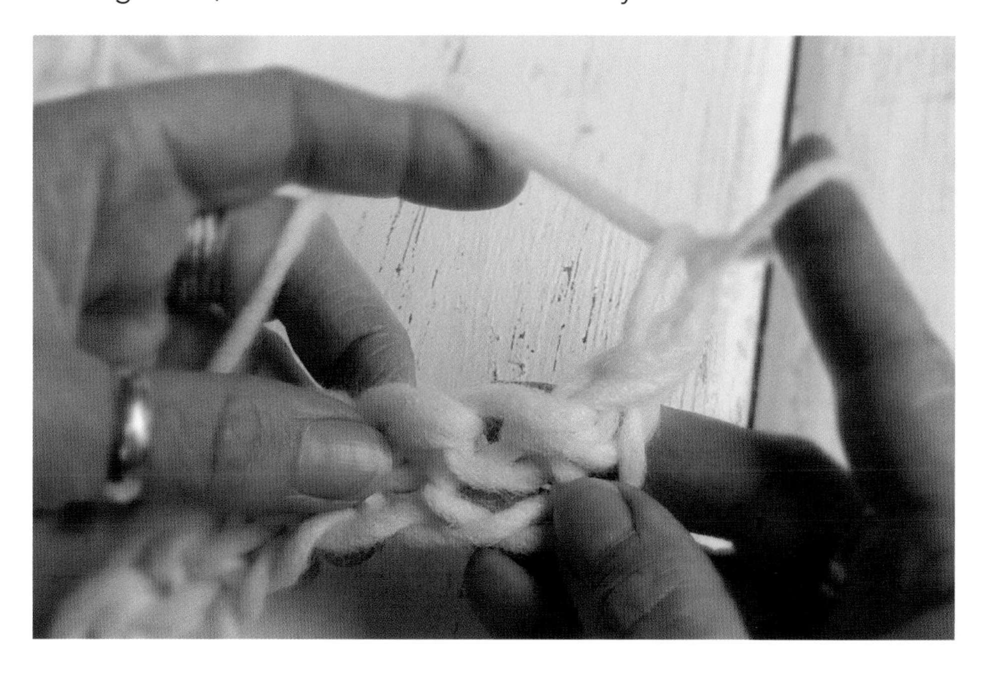

12. Put your right index finger through the second stitch in the space under the 'V' shape as indicated.

13. Continue to yarn over and bring the wool through the hole to make two loops on your finger, before pinching through both of these, grabbing the yarn and pulling it all the way through to make a stitch.

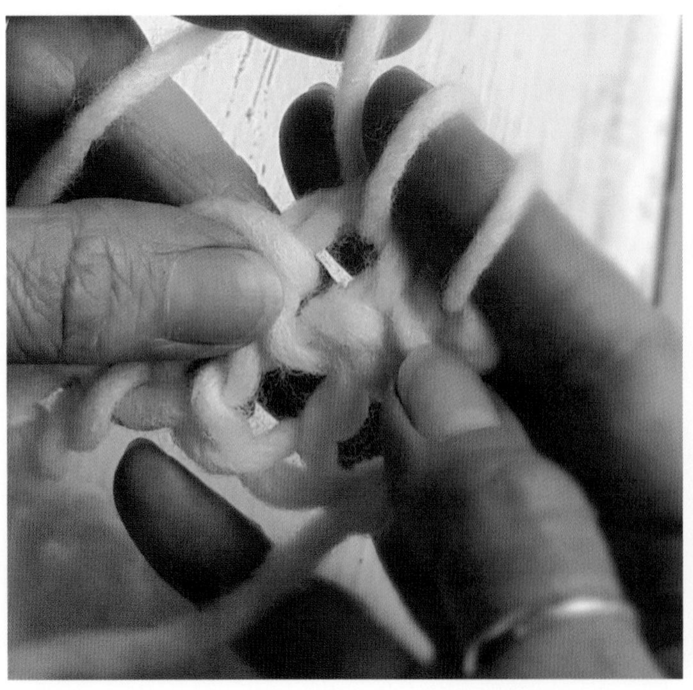

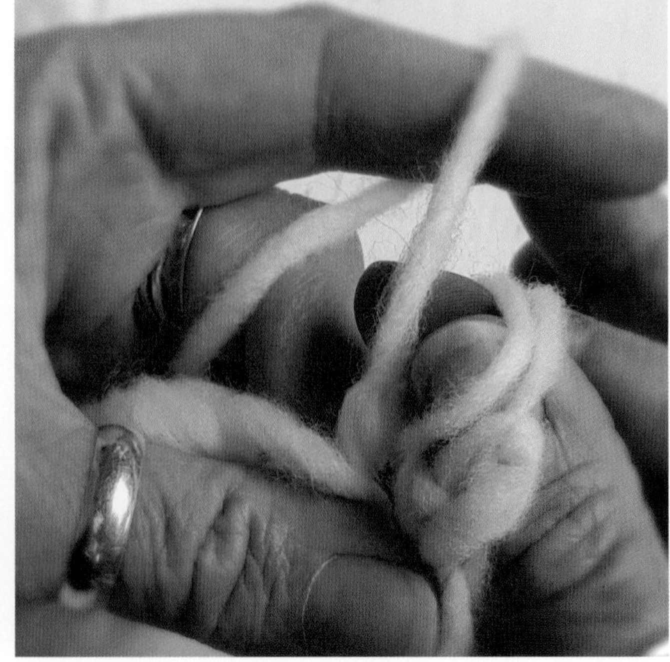

14. Repeat stages 10 to 13 until the work measures about 20cm in width.

15. To finish off, cut the working yarn off with about 50cm excess, pull it through the loop on your finger and pull tight. Use this to stitch the ends together to make an infinity scarf (putting a twist in the work before you sew it can give an interesting effect) before weaving in the other loose end. Alternatively you can leave the ends unsewn to make a traditional scarf.

UPCYCLED NORDIC CUSHION COVER

Have you ever loved a Christmas jumper so dearly that you were bereft when the moths had their wicked way with it? Well, fret no more as here we have four ways to breathe new life into your favourite Nordic sweater. I have to admit I am not a great one for measuring and pinning things out accurately when using a sewing machine, so these projects generally involve the most basic of measurements and the use of a hot glue gun.

The fabric from the front and back of the sweater is used to make an envelope-style cushion cover, and to ensure it is nice and plump it should measure 5cm less than the insert. For this cushion I used a 40cm pillow so the final cover measured 35cm. Be warned, once the jumper has been cut it can start to fray uncontrollably, so here the side pieces were sewn to the correct dimensions before the fabric was trimmed.

Materials

A preloved jumper (the bigger the better. If you can't bear to cut up yours, they are easily found on auction websites)

- Cushion pillow
- Sewing machine and thread
- 35mm wooden button

- 3mm 4-strand macramé cord
- Tape measure
- Scissors
- Pins

1. Cut the jumper up the sides, along the neck seam and round the front collar. Repeat for the back.

2. Putting the right sides of the fabric together, stitch a line about a centimetre in along the bottom edge of the jumper to form the first seam of the cushion cover.

3. Lay your cushion insert on top of the two pieces so the bottom edge is flush with the stitched seam in order to work out your measurements.

4. Fold the front section of the jumper down over the pillow and trim in a straight line so it reaches about halfway down. Turn this cut edge over twice (starting with wrong sides together) and stitch in place. This will be the longer piece of the envelope, which makes both the cushion back and the front flap.

5. Cut the neck piece from the other side of the jumper in a straight line, so it is 5cm shorter than your cushion. Fold over twice and hem, wrong sides together.

6. With the right sides of the cushion cover together, first fold the longer back piece down so it makes an envelope shape 35cm tall, and then fold the shorter piece up (insert the cushion briefly just to check everything is fitting nicely).

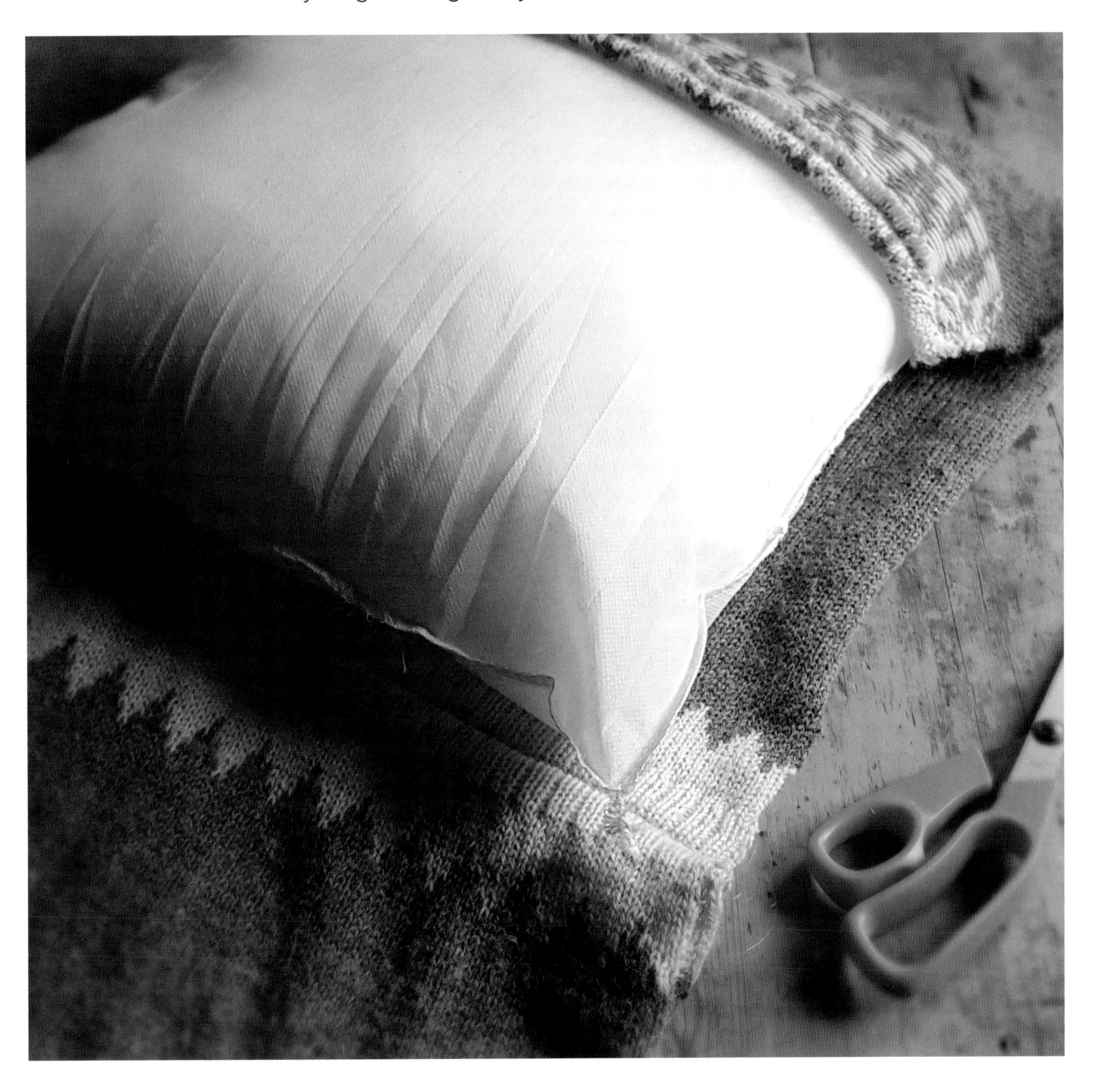

7. Using a felt tip, mark at the top and bottom where the side seams are going to go, ensuring that they are no more than 35cm apart. Pin in place, then sew down one of the seams; sew back the other way about a centimetre further out to stop the seam fraying, then trim with scissors.

8. Repeat for the second side seam.

9. Turn the cover inside out and insert the pillow.

10. Cut a 10cm length of the macramé cord. Fold it in half and stitch to the inside of the cushion flap, ensuring that the loop is big enough to fit over your button.

11. Stitch on the button, plump up the cushion and then reflect on the glory of your handiwork.

RECYCLED BOTTLE BANGLES

These fun bangles can be made in just a few minutes using strips cut from the top of the jumper sleeves, a glue gun and a plastic drinks bottle. Try and find a bottle with a diameter of about 8cm, then you will have plenty of room to slip the bracelet over your wrist without it being too large and floppy.

Materials

- Plastic squash bottle
- Jumper sleeves
- 8mm wooden buttons
- Hot glue gun
- Iron

1. Cut your sections from the rinsed plastic bottle using sharp scissors; I would suggest a minimum width of at least 2cm as this will give you enough room to fold the fabric over and glue it down neatly. Trim off any little spiky bits.

2. Set your iron to a medium heat and then gently rub the plastic ring over it in a circular motion. As the plastic heats up it will start to curve inwards, giving you a lovely rounded edge. The centre of the iron will be much hotter, so keep turning the ring so it melts evenly.

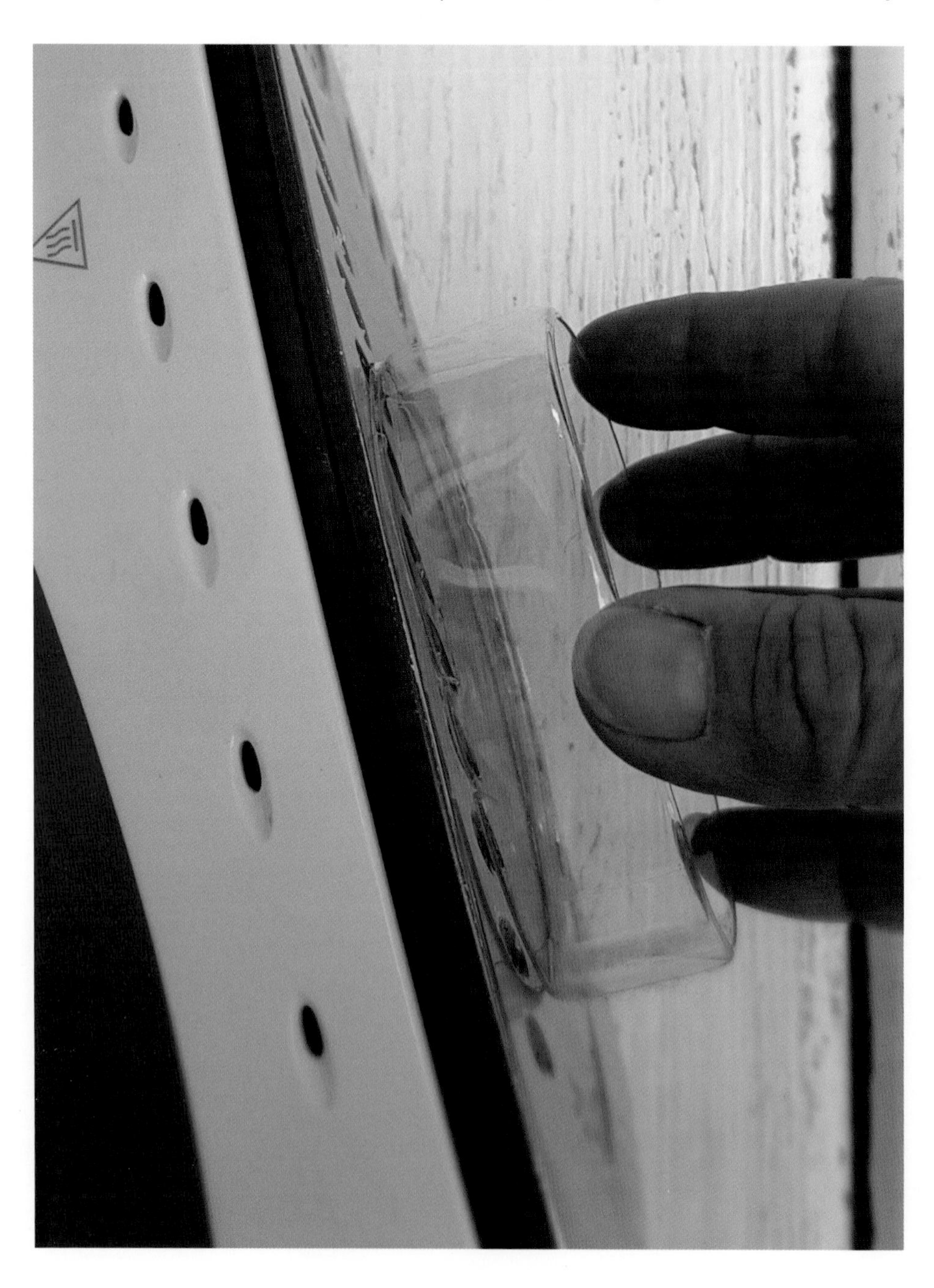

3. Once you have a smooth edge, turn the bangle over and repeat with the other side.

4. Cut a section of jumper that measures three times the width of the bangle, and 1cm longer.

5. Set your glue gun to a low heat, as too hot a temperature can melt the plastic bangle (as I found out early on).

6. Working in small sections, apply a short line of adhesive down the centre of the outside of the bangle, then press it on to the centre of the fabric, wrong side up. Keep rolling and gluing until the bangle is covered.

7. Repeat the process on the inside of the bracelet, adding a thin line of glue down the centre and folding one edge in to fix it down firmly.

8. Turn the bangle around and glue down the second edge.

9. Apply a scant amount of adhesive to the inside of the overlapped seam and press down to secure, then glue on the wooden buttons to cover the join.

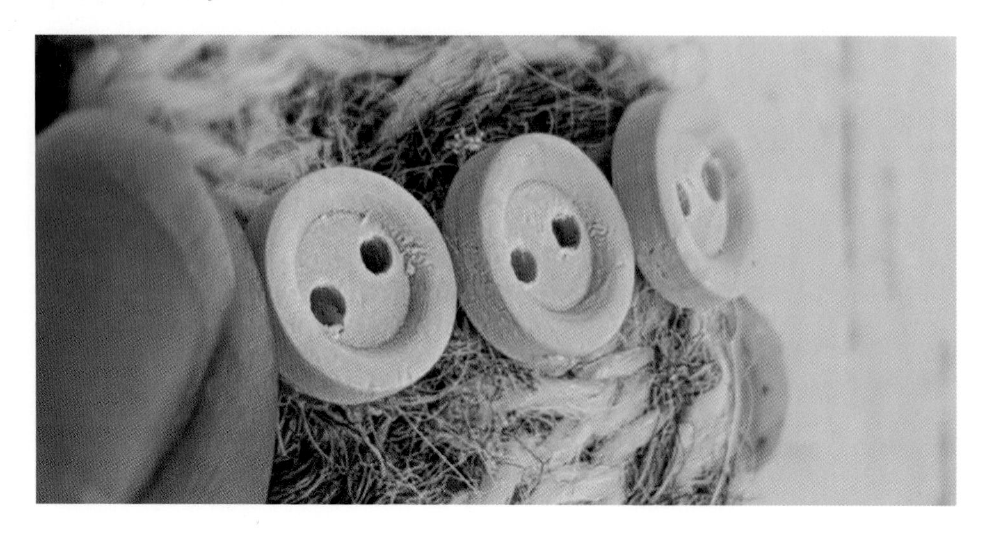

QUICK AND EASY CHRISTMAS BAUBLES

It struck me, as I was gaily hacking up the jumper to make the cushion cover for this project, that the most attractive part of Nordic and Fair Isle sweaters is often around the neckline, and that there had to be a good way of using up this area of fabric effectively. The result was these pretty little baubles, created in just a few minutes with tiny embroidery hoops.

Materials

- 8cm bamboo embroidery hoops
- 10mm grosgrain ribbon
- Jumper fabric
- Hot glue gun
- Felt

1. Take the centre ring out of the hoop and use it as a template to cut a circle of felt the same size.

2. Stretch your jumper fabric over the central ring and place the outer ring back over it.

3. Tighten up the little screw to ensure it fits securely.

4. Snip around the outside with scissors, leaving a 2cm border, then run a ring of hot glue around the edge of the fabric.

5. Fold the border in and press down to fix it in place.

6. Feed a 25cm length of ribbon through the hole under the screw and then knot to make a hanging loop.

7. Glue the felt circle over the back to hide any tatty areas.

8. Tie a bow in the ribbon and glue it on to the front of the ornament to hide the screw fixing.

WONDERFUL WRIST WARMERS

Now let's turn our attention to those lovely patterned sleeves. I am a huge fan of wrist warmers, and am rarely to be seen without them from September to May; however, I am also prone to losing them, so this a great way of not only using up the last of our gorgeous sweater, but also ensuring one still has circulation in one's fingers on those icy winter walks. They can be made as long or as short as you like; shorter ones are perfect for winter typing in chilly offices, whereas longer ones guarantee no more icy draughts up your coat sleeves.

1. Measure your hand against the sweater cuff. I have fairly small hands and find a width of 8cm at the cuff is perfect, this will be the part that covers your knuckles.

2. Decide how long you would like your wrist warmers to be, then turn the first sleeve inside out and mark a rectangle 8cm along the length of the sleeve, using the straighter edge as the thumb seam.

3. Fold the shorter side over and hem to make the elbow end of the warmer, then stitch up the inside seam, zipping up and down a couple of times with the machine to ensure the fabric cannot fray too much. Cut off the excess.

4. To make a thumb hole, lay the sleeve on the table, still wrong side out, and measure your hand against the fabric so the cuff rests over your knuckles. Snip a 2cm cut where your thumb will go, then fold the material over and hand stitch in place to make a neat edge.

5. Repeat with the second sleeve.

FELT BALL COASTERS

I love working with felt during the winter; warm to the touch and pleasingly tactile, these felted coasters will add a pop of colour to any Christmas stocking. The felt balls are available online in a variety of colours and sizes. Here I have used felt balls with 1.5cm diameter to make a stable base for a cup; any bigger and your precious coffee is likely to rock about alarmingly.

There is no right or wrong way to stitch the balls together, you are just trying to ensure that each one is connected to at least two others in order to make the project as durable as possible. To begin with, the balls are threaded into a long snake; this not only adds an extra layer of stability but makes attaching them to the coaster so much easier. The only tricky part to this project is remembering

when to change direction. If you carry on sewing the snake into a spiral ad infinitum, at some point the snake will run out and the shape will be uneven. For this reason we are actually making a hexagon, not a circle, so by changing direction it gives you a new corner to work from.

I tend to use invisible thread as coloured stitches will be glaringly obvious on the outside edge. You may also find a thimble useful as some balls tend to be denser than others and it can be harder to get the needle through. Leftover balls can be strung into garlands using embroidery thread, or sewn into bracelets with jewellery elastic as another quick gift.

Materials

- Long needle
- invisible thread/fishing line
- 36 x 1.5cm felt balls

1. Thread the balls on to a long, doubled piece of thread and knot one end firmly, leaving the other end free; this will allow you to slide them up and down and fit them into the work more easily.

2. The first felt sphere on the tied end will be the centre of your coaster. Knot a new long piece of thread on to your needle and pass it through the middle of the first and third spheres, and then back through the first one. Make sure the stitches go through the centre as this will ensure your coaster lies flat.

3. Now sew the first ball to the fourth and back again, then to the fifth and so on. Repeat this process until you have made a hexagon of seven balls.

4. Continue stitching backwards and forwards all the way round to make the third row, slotting the spheres in between each other so they fit evenly; you should now have a hexagon with three balls making up each side.

5. Row four involves a change of direction. When your thread is leaving the last ball of row three, skip a ball and then stitch through the next one on the snake.

6. Continue working in the new direction, ensuring each felt shape fits neatly in between two others. Finish off by stitching over a couple of times in between two of the internal balls, so that when you snip off the tail it is hidden, and then repeating the process with the thread from the end of your initial snake.

DIP-DYED KEY TASSELS

The origin of the term 'macramé' dates back to Arabic weavers, who made intricate fringes to edge their migramah or embroidered veils. This art of knotting string was particularly popular in the 1970s (particularly in owl-format), but is now making something of a comeback as people turn to natural fibres for their crafts. Cream, mustard and grey colours of yarn all suit themselves perfectly to a neutral Scandinavian palette, and the addition of wooden beads fits in wonderfully with that log-cabin feel.

Before you embark on your first project, I would suggest practising the required knot a few times before you start, just so you can get used to the tension (both literal and mental) of working with long pieces of string. (I say this as someone whose cat always likes to get deeply involved in the crafting process; in fact, as I was making the keyrings for the photograph I had to make her a little one of

her own to play with, just so she would leave me alone for twenty minutes.) After a few centimetres, you will quickly see how tightly you need to pull the working threads to get consistently sized knots and therefore a neater finish.

Both these designs are made using 3mm cotton macramé yarn; not only is it soft and pleasurable to work with, it is easily undone in case of the odd error and won't make your fingers sore over extended periods of time.

Materials

- 3mm 4-strand macramé cord
- 12mm wooden beads with 4mm hole
- 25mm split keyrings
- Darning needle
- Food colouring
- White vinegar
- Old toothbrush or comb

Spiral keyring

1. To make a twisted key tassel, cut two 100cm lengths of cord and tie two lark's head knots (also known as cow hitches) on to a split ring. Do this by folding one of the lengths in half, placing it in front of the split ring and pushing it through.

2. Now feed the two ends through that loop and pull tight.

3. Repeat with the other cord.

4. To tie your spiral knots, take the left working cord, pass it over the top of the two filler cords then behind the right working length.

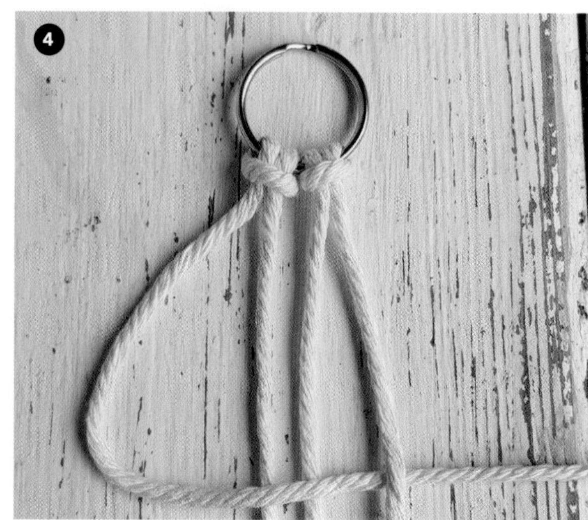

5. Pick up the right working cord, take it behind the fillers and pass it through the loop that has been formed on the left, from back to front.

6. Gently pull the ends to form your first knot.

7. Continue until you reach the desired length of knot work. Beads can be added in by feeding both filler cords one by one through the hole using a darning needle, then continuing to knot.

8. At this stage you can just tie the work off in a knot before fluffing the tassel, but wrapping the cord looks much neater and ensures the tassel doesn't lie at a funny angle.

9. Wrapping knots are a great way of bundling cords together neatly. Cut a 40cm length of cord and hold one end above where

your knotted work ends. Take the long end down and back up to form a loop, ensuring it is the same length as the rest of your tassel.

10. Pinch the top firmly in your left hand to hold the cords in place, then begin to wrap the cord around the bundle until you have reached the desired length.

11. Feed the wrapping cord through the bottom loop, then gently pull the cord that is still poking out of the top; the bottom loop should close up leaving you with a neat finish. Snip off both ends then brush the tassel using either a toothbrush or comb. Trim with scissors.

Square knot keyring

1. To make a square knotted keyring, tie two 100cm cords to your split ring, again using lark's head knots (as above).

2. A square knot is very similar to the spiral knot, but instead of always starting with the left cord, you will alternate the same manoeuvre from the right to keep the work lying flat.

3. Pick up your left working cord, pass it over the top of the fillers then behind the right working cord (as above).

4. Take the right working cord, take it behind the fillers and pass it through the loop that has been formed on the left, from back to front. Pull gently to tighten.

5. Once you have pulled the ends tight, pick up your right working cord and pass it over the top of the fillers and behind the left cord.

6. Now take the left cord, take it behind the fillers and through the loop you have made, passing it from back to front, then tighten.

7. Add in beads as you fancy by threading them on to the two filler cords, and continue until you have reached your desired length. Finish off by wrapping the cord bundle, as above.

Dyed keyrings

1. Pour 100ml of hot water into a glass or ceramic bowl and stir in two tablespoons of white vinegar, to act as a fixative.

2. Add in 20–30 drops of food colouring and mix to combine.

3. Put your keyring under the tap and soak it thoroughly, then squeeze out all the excess water.

4. Dip the bottom centimetre into the food colouring and then take it out quickly; it will spread much further than you think! Leave for ten minutes or so, then rinse under the tap. If you would like to add a little deeper colour at the base, add a few more drops of colouring to the water and repeat the procedure, just dipping the very tips of the tails into the liquid.

5. Rinse and leave to dry before brushing out the tassels and trimming neatly.

CHRISTMAS TREE BODY SCRUB

The lead up to Christmas can be hectic, with plans for cooking, gift-shopping and decorating seeming to fill every waking moment, so what would make a lovelier festive gift for a dear one than a home-made spa basket? Pop in a jar of Christmas Tree Body Scrub, a fluffy facecloth and a nourishing lotion candle and you have the perfect present for a tired friend. Leftover lavender buds from these recipes can be used to fill muslin teabags to slip under pillows or for scenting linen drawers.

Before I started making this scrub, I often resembled an elderly

lizard during the colder months. Now, however, with its exfoliating texture and nourishing properties, I rise from bathing soft and sleek, like a young otter. The best way to apply it is to run a warm bath, then splash water over your skin; apply the scrub in a circular motion before immersing yourself in the steaming waters and letting all those salts and essential oils do their work.

Pine needles are exceptionally high in Vitamin C and have long been used for traditional remedies, and here they add a little colour and texture to the scrub, along with the tiny purple buds of dried lavender. Pine, spruce and fir needles can all be used, but please make sure you identify them correctly and do not use yew, all parts of which are poisonous. For this reason I would therefore suggest you discreetly sneak a few needles from the back of your Christmas tree, which is likely to be Norway Spruce, Nordmann or Douglas Fir, or Scots Pine.

Rich in magnesium and renowned for their therapeutic properties, Dead Sea salts will buff away dry skin and relax aching muscles, while coconut and sweet almond oil soften and moisturise. The mixture will last for months if not contaminated with water, so if you are giving a jar away as a gift, tie on a little wooden spoon for the recipient so they can scoop it out easily without having to use wet hands.

A number of caveats: the scrub may leave your bath or shower very slippery so do take care, and essential oils should not be used if pregnant or under the age of 12. Caution should be used if you have underlying health conditions; do not use the salt scrub on your face or delicate areas. With regards to shelf life, the scrub should last as long as the shortest 'use by' date marked on your ingredients. Store it in a cool dark place to preserve the fragrance of the essential oils.

Ingredients (enough to make 1 x 500ml jar)

- 450g fine Dead Sea salts
- 110g of coconut oil
- 3tbsp sweet almond oil
- 1tbsp dried lavender
- 1tbsp fresh conifer needles
- 25 drops of essential oil (5 pine, 5 bergamot, 5 frankincense and 10 lavender)
- 500ml Kilner jar
- Small wooden spoon

1. Wash your pine needles thoroughly and allow them to dry (just in case your Christmas tree has been sprayed with any chemicals). Chop them finely so you have enough to fill a tablespoon.

2. Melt the coconut oil and the sweet almond oil together in a small pan and then allow to cool.

3. Using a small glass container, mix together the essential oils before adding a little of the melted coconut and almond oils and swirling them around (this premixing ensures they blend thoroughly).

4. Measure the salts into a large bowl, add the chopped needles and dried lavender heads and then pour over the oil mixture, stirring well to combine.

5. Tip the salts into the storage jar and leave in a dark place for a week for the essential oils to infuse, before labelling and tying on a wooden spoon with a pretty ribbon.

LAVENDER AND BERGAMOT BATH SOAK

Even though they are called 'salts', Epsom salts are not actually sodium chloride. In fact they are actually magnesium sulphate crystals, and are famed for their ability to soothe tired and aching muscles as well as helping to detoxify the body. Add these to the rich mix of over twenty minerals found in Dead Sea salts and you have a wonderful combination for a perfectly luxurious bath. Bicarbonate of soda (also known as baking soda) is added as well, to give a little touch of silkiness to the water, calm irritated skin and act as a mild antiseptic.

The addition of dried flower petals can give a lovely texture and colour to the appearance of the soak, but they do tend to clog up the bath plughole, so if you have a particularly fastidious friend you might wish to leave them out. If you are organised you can harvest rose blooms, marigold petals and lavender buds (before they flower) in the summer; dry them in the sun and keep them in sealed containers ready for your Christmas projects (or panic buy them online in early December, like me).

As ever, it is important that you only use skin-safe essential oils, so here I have included the most relaxing of them all. Lavender is said to not only calm the mind and promote sleep, but is also full of antioxidants that are great for the skin, while bergamot is the oil of cheerfulness, uplifting one's spirits and alleviating stress.

Ingredients (enough to fill 1 x 500ml jar, or 3 x 175ml glass bottles)

- 300g Dead Sea salts
- 150g Epsom salts
- 50g bicarbonate of soda
- 15 drops of lavender essential oil
- 10 drops of bergamot essential oil
- Lavender buds, dried rose or calendula petals
- A few drops of food colouring (optional)

1. Weigh the salts and soda and place them in a large ceramic mixing bowl (I always give the bicarbonate of soda a good old squish with the back of a metal spoon to smooth out any lumps).

2. Sprinkle the essential oils evenly over the mixture and then stir thoroughly to combine. If you would like to create salts in pretty pastel shades, add a

Lavender and Bergamot Bath Salts
Lavender and Bergamot Bath Salts
Lavender and Bergamot Bath Salts

couple of drops of food colouring at this stage and mix again.

3. Excess moisture in your mixture can sometimes cause the salts to clump together. While this is not a problem if you are going to pack them into wide mouth Kilner jars or glass containers, it can sometimes be an issue if you wish to present them in attractive narrow-necked bottles. If you find this to be a problem, line a baking sheet with tinfoil and spread the salts out in an even layer. Bake at 75°C for fifteen minutes; stir every five minutes to dry them out thoroughly then leave on the sheet until cold.

4. Add any dried flower petals to the mixture at this stage, then using a piece of paper as a funnel, pour the salts into your prepared containers. If you are feeling particularly artistic, layering the petals in as you pour them in provides a glorious little pop of colour.

5. Fix on the lids and leave for forty-eight hours for the aromas to blend, then store in a cool dark place to stop the light-sensitive essential oils degrading.

LAVENDER LOTION CANDLE

Not only are candles an easy way to add a hyggelig glow to your evening, but with this clever recipe you can also use them as a body lotion or massage oil. Lotion candles are easy to make in batches using soy wax and can be scented with skin-safe essential oils for both fabulous fragrance and a soothing effect on mind and body. Soy wax melts at a much lower temperature than paraffin wax so is fine to use on skin when liquid; when mixed with nourishing sweet almond and coconut oils, it is a splendid way to moisturise dry hands or pamper tired feet. I tend to collect any interesting little glass yoghurt jars, tiny coffee cups and mini cheesecake dishes throughout the year as these make excellent candle jars and are often about 100ml, making it easy to scale up the recipe.

Once a candle has burnt down to about a centimetre it is no longer safe to use, but any empty candle jars can easily be reused for this project. I once spent a dreadful afternoon chipping wax out of my U-bend with a potato peeler so heartily recommend you get rid of as much old wax as possible before washing them. Line a baking tray with tinfoil, and preheat the oven to about 175°C. Stand the candle jars upside down on the tray then bake for about fifteen minutes, allowing the wax to melt and run out. Leave on a heat-proof surface to cool down before giving the jars a quick wash in hot soapy water.

Please note that the lotion candles will be softer than the standard variety, and as I generally make them in the depths of a dark, cold English winter (and as coconut oil liquefies at a temperature of 24°C) they tend to solidify nicely. However, if you are making them in summer or in much warmer climes, I would suggest swapping the coconut oil for an equal weight of shea butter. It is not absorbed into the skin quite as quickly but makes a great alternative to help your candles set.

For a warming massage, light the candle as normal and let it burn for around fifteen minutes; once you have a pool of melted wax, blow the candle out and let it cool for a couple of minutes before either dipping in your fingers or pouring some into the palm of your hand. Rub into skin for a pampering experience. As ever, please do not leave a lit candle unattended, and keep well away from children and pets.

Ingredients

(this makes enough to fill 1 x 100ml small glass jar, so measure how many millilitres you need to fill your candle holders and scale the recipe up as necessary)

- 50g soy wax
- 25g coconut oil
- 25g sweet almond oil
- 25 drops of lavender oil

Materials

- Metal jug and saucepan
- Glue gun or glue dots
- Pair of chopsticks or pencils
- Elastic bands
- Pre-tabbed and waxed cotton soy candle wick

1. Prepare your glass jars. Fix the metal tab on the wick in place at the centre of your candle glass using either a glue dot or a blob of adhesive from your hot glue gun.

2. Secure the chopsticks/pencils at either end using elastic bands, and then slip them over the top of the wick. This will ensure that the wick will remain centred once you pour the wax in. (If you have

bought a candle kit and are faced with a bundle of string and some metal bases, don't panic. Cut the wick into lengths 2cm longer than the top of your candle. When the soy wax has melted in step 3, dip the lengths into the wax with tweezers then lay them out to dry on a piece of paper, straightening them out as they cool. Once they are firm, thread them through the metal sustainers and crimp with pliers to secure in place.)

3. Place the wax in the metal jug, and set this in a pan of simmering water over a low heat. Once the soy has melted, add the coconut and almonds oils and stir thoroughly until dissolved.

4. Remove from the heat and allow to cool for about ten minutes before adding the lavender oil and stirring once again (adding any essential oils too quickly will affect their fragrance).

5. Carefully pour the mixture into the candle glass and leave for 4–5 hours to cool down (it will take longer than a candle made of pure wax)

6. Trim the wick to about half a centimetre and leave for a couple of days for the scent to infuse. Once you have made the candles it is a good idea to put a lid on your jars (if they have one) or cover with cling film to preserve the fragrance until you give them as a gift.

MINI LOTION MELTS

Any leftover candle wax mixture can be made into sweet little lotion bars very easily. Silicone ice cube trays or doubled-up paper muffin cases make ideal moulds; however, my mother has a lifelong addiction to mince pies, so I find this a great way to recycle all those aluminium tart tins she starts accumulating from October onwards. The metal cases also make handy dishes to present and store them in (the average mince pie tin will hold about 100ml of the liquid lotion).

1. Sprinkle lavender buds, rose or calendula petals into the base of your moulds. Carefully pour any remaining mixture into the mince pie tins, using a chopstick to arrange the floating petals to your satisfaction.

2. Set aside overnight to cool and infuse, then pop out of the moulds if you are using them.

3. Keep one by the kitchen sink, warm between your hands and rub in those fabulous melted moisturisers to soften and protect skin after all that Christmas washing up. I keep one by my bed and apply it just before bedtime, to soothe and prevent chapped winter fingers; it also works miracles on feet and elbows.

CHAPTER FOUR

CHRISTMAS COMFORT FOOD

Christmas in our house mostly revolves around food, whether it be the planning, the shopping or the consumption. From soft and fluffy cinnamon buns for breakfast on Christmas Eve to a crisp joint of pork slathered in rich brown gravy later on that evening, it is the meals that really are the focus of everyone's attention, as we sit down to enjoy each other's company, play some games and then slip into a quiet sense of contentment after the last drop of akvavit has been drained.

OVERNIGHT KANELSNEGLE (CINNAMON SNAILS)

Waking up to the prospect of a tummy full of warm, freshly baked cinnamon buns surely has to be one of the highlights of a cold Sunday morning. These fabulously sticky, fragrant rolls are not only easy to make ahead, but can be popped in the freezer and baked when needed, making them an invaluable part of your Very Organised Christmas.

This recipe will make roughly twenty-four buns; as they are best eaten warm from the oven, I tend to put half in the fridge overnight for breakfast the next morning, and freeze the rest on a baking sheet lined with greaseproof paper. Once they are frozen solid, pack them into ziplock bags and put them back in the freezer, where they will keep happily for up to a month; allow to defrost overnight in the fridge, and then prove and bake as usual.

The time taken for the dough to rise for the first time is very temperature dependent. In summer, I have had the mixture double in size in an hour and a half, but in winter it can take twice this, so it is best to complete this stage in the fairly early evening so it doesn't interfere with your bedtime.

Ingredients

For the dough

- 500g plain flour
- 10 cardamom pods
- 2 sachets of fast-action dried yeast (14g)
- 200ml milk
- 50g butter, roughly chopped into cubes
- 2 eggs
- ¼tsp salt

For the filling

- 125g butter, softened
- 75g brown sugar
- 75g caster sugar
- 1tbsp ground cinnamon

For the glaze

- 1 egg, beaten
- Pearl sugar (smashed-up sugar cubes will work if you cannot source any pearl sugar, which are larger granules than usual that retain their shape when baked)

1. Ground cardamom can lose its potency very quickly so it is preferable to use the pods. Crush them in a pestle and mortar (or bash them with the end of a rolling pin).

2. Place the pods and their seeds in a small pan with the milk and butter and warm over a low heat until the milk is just about steaming. Remove from the stove and swirl around until the butter has melted.

3. To make the dough, combine the flour, yeast and salt in a large bowl, or in your kitchen mixer fitted with a dough hook.

4. Make a well in the centre of the bowl, then strain the milk mixture, through a sieve, over the flour, discarding the cardamom pods.

5. Add the eggs and mix to combine. Knead the dough either by hand or in your kitchen mixer with a dough hook fitted. It will be quite sticky, but don't be tempted to add any extra flour at this stage as it will make the buns dry. By hand it will probably take about ten minutes to achieve a smooth and bouncy dough, or about five minutes in the mixer.

6. Rub a thin layer of oil over a clean bowl, shape your dough into

a ball and leave it to rest, nicely nestled and covered with a sheet of cling film (I have an elderly hotel shower cap which suits the purpose admirably). Prove until it has doubled in size and pings back nicely when you prod it.

7. Meanwhile, line two roasting tins with greaseproof paper, then mix the filling ingredients in a small bowl until thoroughly combined.

8. Once your dough has risen to your satisfaction, roll it out into an oblong roughly 50cm by 30cm, with the long edge facing towards you.

9. Using the back of a large spoon, smear the doughy rectangle with the buttery, crunchy filling, taking care to push it right to the edges (nobody wants a dry bit).

10. Starting with the long edge, roll the dough up into a sausage. At this stage you can either cut it with a sharp knife into 2cm slices, or, my preferred method, using baker's twine or strong thread (you can even use unwaxed dental floss). Pass the thread under the sausage at about 2cm in, then pull the furthest end towards you and the nearest one away, thus (hopefully), cutting the snails neatly.

11. Lay them into your prepared tins with the whirly sides facing up (discard the very ends of the sausage, or bake separately for private consumption), then cover tightly with cling film and pop them in the fridge overnight (or straight into the freezer).

12. To bake the buns, remove from the fridge and allow them to rise a second time for 1–2 hours. Once they have puffed up again, brush them with beaten egg, sprinkle with pearl sugar and place in paper muffin cases.

13. Preheat the oven to 180°C. Bake for 8–12 minutes until golden brown; they tend to catch quite easily, so check them every minute or so in the final stages.

14. I find them sweet enough already, but if you would like to make an icing, simply mix 3 tablespoons of milk and 150g of icing sugar together (adding a little more liquid if necessary) to make a runny icing about the consistency of single cream. Allow the buns to cool then drizzle over the top with a fork.

OVERNIGHT RYE BREAD

Scandinavian rye bread is a terribly more-ish loaf; high in protein, dense and with a tightly packed crumb, it is well-suited to the elaborate open sandwich toppings favoured by Danes. Many recipes call for a sourdough starter, but as it is rare that I can think four to six days ahead to create the necessary starter, this overnight recipe is a favourite. As there is very little gluten content in rye, it doesn't have to be kneaded like white breads, and just requires a thorough mixing at the start. This can either be done by hand (if you are feeling energetic), otherwise five minutes in a food mixer with a dough hook attachment will do the trick nicely.

The great thing about this bread is that you don't have to hang about all day while it proves; simply mix up a batch while you are pottering about in the kitchen in the evening and then you can bake it the next morning. Purists will tell you that rye bread needs to be left to rest for 5–6 hours before slicing and serving, but I have yet to manage this.

Ingredients (enough to make 1 loaf, filling a 900ml loaf tin)

- 250g rye flour
- 250g strong white flour
- 350ml water, warm to the touch
- 50g sunflower seeds
- 2tbsp melted butter or vegetable oil
- 1tbsp black treacle
- 1tbsp muscovado sugar
- 1tbsp cocoa
- 2tsp caraway seeds
- 1½ tsp salt
- ½tsp dried fast-action yeast
- Sunflower seeds or oats, to sprinkle on top

1. Place the rye and strong flour in a large bowl and add the sugar, salt, seeds, caraway, yeast and salt.

2. Make a well in the centre and add the oil and treacle (if you measure the oil out first and then use the same spoon for the treacle, it will slide off much more easily).

3. Pour in the warm water and mix thoroughly to combine; the resulting dough will be soft and slightly sticky, and much rougher than a traditional white bread dough.

4. Cover the bowl with a piece of oiled cling film and leave overnight to prove for 14–16 hours.

5. In the morning the dough should have risen and will have a puffy appearance. Grease a 900ml loaf tin and dust the bottom with a little rye flour. Scrape the dough into the tin, pushing it carefully into the corners, then smooth the top down with wet fingers. Sprinkle on a few more seeds or some porridge oats if you fancy.

6. Leave for another 1–2 hours to rise; the loaf will puff up slightly but don't expect anything dramatic. A fingertip poked in gently should result in a dip which holds its shape.

7. Preheat the oven to 180°C and bake on the centre shelf for 40–45 minutes; if you tip it out of the tin and rap on the bottom it should sound vaguely hollow.

8. Leave to cool before serving with a thick smear of butter, an artful draping of smoked salmon and a sprinkling of dill. (Thickly buttered bread is known as tandsmør (tooth-butter), which means it is so thickly applied it shows teeth marks when bitten.)

AGURKESALAT (CUCUMBER SALAD)

This easy pickled cucumber salad recipe adds a lovely fresh taste to any open sandwiches or pork dish; serve with hot dogs, roast pork, burgers or even prawn salad. My grandmother always said that you should cut the cucumber as thinly as possible so you can see daylight through the slices.

Ingredients

- 1 English cucumber
- 250ml cup of white vinegar (although I often use cider vinegar or whatever I can find in the cupboard)
- 200g white sugar
- 250ml cup of boiling water
- 15 peppercorns
- 1tsp coriander seeds
- ½tsp of salt
- 2 sprigs of dill, roughly chopped (1 teaspoon of dried dill will also work well)

1. Slice the cucumber as thinly as possible.

2. Whisk together the vinegar, boiling water and sugar until the sugar has dissolved.

3. Add the salt, spices and herbs, stir and allow to cool.

4. Place the thinly sliced cucumbers in a large glass jar and pour over the marinade, then store in the fridge for at least three hours for the flavours to mingle.

5. This will keep in a Kilner jar for a week in the fridge.

REMOULADE

Remoulade is a thick, yellow and utterly ubiquitous Danish condiment, served on everything from breaded fried fish to hot dogs, burgers and smørrebrød. Sweeter than mayonnaise but with a touch of acid from the pickled elements, it is delicious when slathered over pretty much any meat or fish.

I usually buy a few bottles every time I place an online order for Scandinavian ingredients, but this recipe takes just moments to knock up for a cold table or special occasions. Once you have combined the basic ingredients, I would urge you to fiddle with it and make changes as your whim takes you; a squeeze of lemon juice goes beautifully with prawns and a pinch of curry powder makes a great accompaniment to chicken salad. Please don't bother with going to any effort by making the mayonnaise; shop-bought is fine.

Ingredients

- 3tbsp mayonnaise
- 2tbsp chopped fresh white cabbage
- 1tbsp chopped sweet pickled gherkin
- ½tbsp chopped capers
- 1tsp Dijon mustard
- 1tsp sugar
- ¼tsp salt
- Chives, to garnish

1. Drain the gherkins and capers and pat dry with kitchen towel, before chopping them as finely as you can.

2. Shred the cabbage and chop into small pieces.

3. Combine the cabbage, gherkin and capers in a small bowl with the other ingredients, before checking the seasoning, and possibly adding a touch more sugar if your tooth runs sweet; shop-bought mayonnaise often contains quite a lot of salt, so I just add a generous twist of black pepper.

4. Leave for an hour or so for the flavours to blend and the sugar to dissolve before dressing with a few chopped chives and placing on your cold table for your guests to help themselves.

SMØRREBRØD (OPEN SANDWICHES)

Smørrebrød (literally 'butter-bread') open sandwiches are little mountains of joy, with both fresh and cooked ingredients beautifully balanced on a piece of buttered rye bread. The most quintessential of Danish lunches, they can be culinary art forms, with presentation just as important as flavour.

For everyday family meals one can just pass round dishes full of

toppings and a basket of bread so everyone can help themselves. However, at Christmas and other important feasts there is a certain protocol involved in eating these, the most glamorous of sandwiches. A knife and fork must always be used (for obvious reasons, when you consider how top-heavy they can get), and there is a certain order in which they must be served; herring is always presented first, then fish such as smoked salmon and prawns. Meats such as frikadeller meatballs, roast beef and pork will follow, then lastly a cheese course, along with much cold lager, ice cold snaps (schnapps) and frequent toasts. Follow up with a little snooze on the sofa.

Ideas for smørrebrød (always butter the bread first to seal it from the more liquid toppings)

- Pickled herring in a curried sauce, with a slice of boiled egg and a tumble of chives over the top
- Smoked salmon, a squeeze of lemon juice and a sprinkling of fresh dill
- Egg mayonnaise with a touch of mustard and a few capers
- Slices of boiled egg, prawn and lettuce
- Roast beef, remoulade and crispy onion
- Roast pork with red cabbage
- Frikadeller with agurkesalat (pickled cucumber salad)
- Blue cheese, pear and chopped walnuts

FRIKADELLER (MEATBALLS)

Frikadeller are small meatballs made from pork, fried until they have a thick, rich dark brown crust. Search online and you will find recipes with the addition of everything from cream and soda water to lighten the mix, to nutmeg for flavour; this is my grandmother's recipe, however, which relies on the onion for taste. She also insisted that you handle the meat as little as possible so as not to compact it, and that they should only be fried in butter to achieve that glorious crust. Pork always needs much more salt than you think, so taste a meatball from the first batch you fry and adjust the seasoning if necessary.

Traditionally served with boiled potatoes and gravy, they taste even better cold the next day with a hefty dollop of creamy potato salad and some agurkesalat as a quick snack.

Ingredients

- 500g minced pork (use mince with a 20 per cent fat content if possible as this will keep the meatballs moist)
- 2tbsp plain flour
- 1 small onion
- 1 egg
- ½tsp salt
- Black pepper
- Butter for frying

1. Grate the onion as finely as possible or blitz it to a puree in a food processor.

2. Mix the pork, onion, flour, egg, salt and a generous grinding of black pepper in a large bowl, stirring with a wooden spoon until combined. The mixture should be quite wet, but add a little extra flour if you think it is too sloppy.

3. Heat a large heavy-based frying pan over a medium heat.

4. Melt 25g of butter in the pan until it is dark brown and bubbling, then turn the heat down a touch. Using two tablespoons, form the meat into oval shapes, trying to touch them as little as possible, then add them to the pan, flattening them slightly.

5. Fry on one side for four to five minutes until a crust has formed and they have changed colour from pink to white about halfway up. Flip them over and cook the other side; you will know the meatballs are cooked when they feel firm to the touch when poked. (If you are frying them in batches, wipe the pan clean with some kitchen paper and add new butter after each batch as the fat quickly becomes quite burnt.)

RØDKÅL (RED CABBAGE)

Red cabbage is traditionally served on Christmas Eve with roast goose, duck or pork as its sweet/sour flavour cuts through the richness of the meat beautifully. It is traditional in our house to make my grandmother's recipe the day before Christmas Eve, as the smell fills the kitchen and gets everyone excited about the party to come. Some recipes omit redcurrant jelly and apples, but I find they give the cabbage a lovely thick, dark red characteristic colour which is missing otherwise.

Ingredients

- 1 red cabbage
- 1 large cooking apple, peeled and chopped roughly
- 200g redcurrant jelly
- 50g butter
- 60ml cider vinegar
- Salt and pepper
- Water

1. Shred the cabbage as finely as possible.

2. Melt the butter in a large heavy-based saucepan (I have an old jam pan I use especially for rødkål as until it starts to cook down, the cabbage takes up a lot of room).

3. Add the cabbage and stir until the butter has been mixed through and the cabbage is glossy.

4. Mix in the vinegar (which keeps the glorious red of the cabbage from turning a rather ghastly blue), apple, and a hefty pinch of seasoning, along with 100ml of cold water. Cover with a lid and simmer over a medium heat for an hour, stirring periodically. If you find it is getting too dry, add another spoonful of water; it should be moistly glossy but not sitting in a pool of liquid.

5. Add the redcurrant jelly and let everything bubble along slowly for another forty-five minutes to an hour, then season and start fiddling with the taste; I often add another couple of spoonfuls of jelly if I find it is not sweet enough. Cook until the cabbage is soft, rich and

thick then leave overnight for the flavours to really develop. Warm gently to serve with your roast pork, or serve cold with your Christmas buffet; it also freezes well, so can be made up to a month ahead.

BRUNEDE KARTOFLER (CARAMELISED POTATOES)

Brunede kartofler (literally brown potatoes) are an essential part of any hyggelig Jul meal. Served as a side dish along with plain boiled potatoes, these sweet and sticky little beasts are a fine accompaniment to both pork and duck.

Waxy small salad potatoes are ideal for caramelising in this way. Please feel free to use fresh ones, but on my constant quest to make Christmas as hassle-free as possible, I confess that actually I use the tinned version (and have been assured by many other Danes that they also prefer to cheat as well). You may find that you have to

cook them in two batches, in which case keep the first crowd of little golden beauties warm in a slow cooker.

Ingredients (serves 6 as side dish)

- 1kg fresh salad potatoes, such as Charlotte (or tinned, if you are feeling lazy)
- 50g butter
- 50g white granulated sugar

1. Boil the fresh potatoes for about fifteen minutes so you can just about poke a fork into them.

2. Leave to cool, before carefully peeling off the skins. Leave them overnight in the fridge if possible, so they can dry out thoroughly. If using tinned, drain them and pat dry with kitchen paper.

3. Spread the sugar over the base of a large frying pan (or cast iron skillet if you have one), place over a medium heat and do not stir. As the sugar melts it will form a wonderful golden caramel.

4. Once the sugar has melted, add the butter to the pan and stir until it foams and forms a syrup.

5. Carefully tip the potatoes into the pan (the syrup will be lava-hot) and cook them for 5–8 minutes, stirring occasionally until the syrup has coated the potatoes and they have caramelised.

FLÆSKESTEG (ROAST PORK)

Such is my love for pork-based dishes that my girlfriends call me 'Pork Girl', and this surely is my favourite of meals, with juicy tender meat and of course the all-important crunchy and burnished crackling. Although traditionally served on Christmas Eve, I cook this all year round on a Sunday evening; leftovers are delicious served in thin slices on rye bread, or fried with potatoes and topped with a fried egg.

Ingredients (serves 6)

- 1.5kg pork loin with rind, unrolled
- 2 carrots
- 1 onion
- Sea salt
- Bay leaves

1. Score the pork rind at ½cm intervals using a craft knife, or ask your butcher to do this for you; it is really important you don't go down as far as the meat, otherwise the juices will rise up and stop the crackling from becoming crisp.

2. Preheat the oven to 250°C and boil the kettle. Lay the pork in the tin with the rind face down (yes, really), pour in boiling water so the rind is covered and then place in the centre of the oven for twenty minutes.

3. Remove the baking tin from the oven and carefully pour away the water. Turn the pork over so the rind is face up, then rub salt into the grooves. Pop a couple of bay leaves into the slices in the skin and pour in 500ml fresh cold water. At this stage it is really important that the pork is lying as flat as possible so that the crackling crisps evenly, so if necessary prop it up with some crumpled tinfoil.

4. Put the tray back in the oven, turn the heat down to 160°C, and cook for another fifty minutes to an hour and ten minutes, or until the internal temperature measures 65°C. Keep topping up the water if necessary.

5. Remove the pork and carefully pour the water into a jug (save this for making gravy). Turn the oven up to 250°C then put the tin back in the centre of the oven for another 10–15 minutes so that the crackling becomes golden and crispy. Do check it occasionally in case it starts to scorch.

6. Remove the joint when a meat thermometer inserted into the pork reaches an internal temperature of 70–75°C and the crackling is cooked to perfection. Let it rest uncovered for 10–15 minutes before carving along the crackling grooves when you are ready to serve (slice too early and the meat can turn grey).

BRUN SOVS (BROWN SAUCE)

Brun sovs is the accompaniment that brings a whole meal together, uniting both meat and potatoes in an unctuous dark brown glory. Gravy is the most essential component of our Christmas meal, and everyone who saunters through the kitchen will taste a spoonful and offer their opinion as to just where you have gone wrong, and what they would do to improve it.

I encourage you to please use this recipe as a starting point before inviting your loved ones to taste a little and then gently critique your gastronomic judgement (preferably while your glasses are steamed up, a timer has just gone off and you attempt to juggle four pans of roasting vegetables … a tiny spoonful more redcurrant jelly, perhaps?).

Ingredients (serves 4–6)

- 60g butter
- 60g plain flour
- 200ml milk
- 600ml of stock, potato water or the liquid from under your roast pork
- Stock cubes
- Gravy browning
- Redcurrant jelly or a sprinkling of sugar
- Salt and pepper

1. Melt the butter in a large heavy-based pan until it is golden brown and foaming.

2. Add the flour and whisk, while continuously adding milk and stirring vigorously to avoid any lumps.

3. Pour in the rest of your liquid. If making frikadeller with boiled potatoes, use the potato cooking water; however, at Christmas the stock from underneath the pork can be used. (Leave it to cool for fifteen minutes or so after you have poured it from the roasting tin, then skim off any excess fat first).

4. Whisk the sauce until smooth. Add a spoonful of redcurrant jelly, crumble in a couple of stock cubes and then let it simmer away gently for a quarter of an hour so that the flour cooks through. Add a couple of drops of gravy browning and then give it a quick taste and adjust the flavourings. I generally add another stock cube or a teaspoon of Marmite and maybe a little more redcurrant jelly.

RISALAMANDE (CHRISTMAS RICE PUDDING WITH WARM CHERRY SAUCE)

This marvellous dessert has to be one of my favourite puddings. It is traditionally eaten on Christmas Eve, and a peeled almond is often hidden in the serving bowl. Whoever finds the almond wins a small prize, although if you do win, you mustn't reveal your victory until the whole dish has been finished.

The rice pudding can be made the day before you need it, which I always feel takes the pressure off slightly. The cooked rice is not too sugary either, with the sweetness coming from the luscious

cherry sauce. I always have to make double quantities as my son likes to eat vast quantities of it while it is still hot, dusted liberally with cinnamon, sugar and finished with a knob of melting salted butter; eaten like this, it is known as risengrod, and is pretty much the epitome of hyggelig comfort puddings.

Ingredients (serves 6)

For the rice pudding

- 750ml whole milk
- 100g pudding rice
- 2 heaped tbsp white sugar
- 250ml double cream
- 1tbsp flaked almonds
- 1 whole peeled almond

For the sauce

- 225g of fresh or frozen cherries
- 3tbsp of sugar
- 250ml of water
- 5 drops of good quality vanilla essence
- 1tbsp cornflour mixed with 125ml of cold water

1. To make the rice pudding, rinse the rice in a sieve to get rid of any excess starch, and allow to drain.

2. Place the rice, milk and sugar in a large, heavy-based saucepan and bring to the boil. Once it is bubbling nicely, turn the heat right down, cover and cook for 30–35 minutes, stirring constantly.

3. As the pudding becomes thicker you will need to pay almost constant attention to make sure it doesn't catch on the bottom; I find a wooden spatula better for this purpose than a spoon as it ensures you don't miss any stray grains of rice lurking on the bottom.

4. Once the rice is tender, taste to check if it is sweet enough for your liking, adding a little more sugar if necessary. Set aside to cool (overnight is fine).

5. Whip the cream into soft peaks, and stir one-third through the rice pudding to loosen it up.

6. Fold through the remaining cream and pile the pudding into a large serving bowl.

7. Poke the almond in, making sure it is well-hidden, then sprinkle with flaked almonds.

8. To make the warm cherry sauce, place 250ml water, sugar and cherries in a saucepan and simmer for about fifteen minutes.

9. Mix the cornflour with 125ml of water to make a smooth paste and pour into the pan.

10. Stir constantly until the fruit thickens into a glossy, silky sauce and serve warm alongside the rice pudding.

ÆBLESKIVER (PANCAKE BALLS)

Æbleskiver literally means 'apple slices' in Danish, and although traditionally made with a chunk of apple inside, they are now more popularly served with jam or compote. The little puffed pancake balls are made in a special pan which is usually cast iron with nine little indentations. They may need a few minutes of quiet practice before you intend serving them to guests for the first time, as there is a knack to turning them so they cook evenly; I find two wooden skewers the best for this.

Ready-made æbleskiver are often bought frozen in Denmark, but once you have made the fluffy fresh version successfully for the first

time you will find that they just don't compare. Serve hot with jam, and a big glass of gløgg. (I must confess that without any regard to respecting the conventions of international cuisine, I have also been known to cook them with a chunk of dark chocolate inside and then roll them in melted butter and cinnamon sugar.)

Theoretically it is a good idea to preheat your oven to around 150°C to keep the æbleskiver warm while you cook the whole batch; in practice they seem to disappear as soon as they come off the stove. If you buy a new iron æbleskiver pan you will need to season it before starting to cook. Wash it thoroughly in hot soapy water, dry well and place on a medium to high heat. Brush with oil. As soon as the oil is smoking, turn the heat off and leave the pan to cool. Wipe with some kitchen paper and then it is ready to use.

Ingredients (makes 16–18)

- 150g plain flour
- 300ml buttermilk
- 50g sugar
- 50g melted butter
- 2 eggs
- ½tsp baking powder
- Pinch of salt
- ½tsp ground cinnamon or ground cardamom
- Extra butter or lard, for frying
- Jam and icing sugar, to serve

1. Sift the flour into a large bowl and stir in the sugar, baking powder, salt and spice.

2. Separate the eggs. Whisk the whites in a separate bowl until glossy and stiff.

3. Beat together the buttermilk, egg yolks and melted butter, then pour into the dry ingredients. Whisk again, until you have a thick, smooth batter.

4. Tip the egg whites on to the batter and then fold gently until combined.

5. Place the pan over a medium heat until it is good and hot then turn the heat down a little. Add a little lump of butter/lard into each hole, allowing it to melt and sizzle.

6. Quickly spoon batter into the holes until each one is just a whisker less than full. After about two minutes the bottom will have formed a shell, so using your skewers hook the half shells and pull them up so they are sticking up at an angle of about 90 degrees.

7. As the batter cooks, keep hooking the shells up and over so that eventually they form balls and seal back on themselves. Keep turning each ball until they are a uniformly golden colour and cooked through; you will be able to feel the balls firm up as they cook, and a skewer poked in discreetly should come out clean.

8. Repeat with the rest of the batter, then dust with icing sugar and serve warm, split open and filled with good quality jam.

9. A couple of useful tips for success: I find it handy to keep a clean tea towel nearby, to wipe the skewers on as necessary. The central hole in the pan will obviously be the hottest, so until you have the knack of turning them, just use the outer ring as it will make the process much less flustering.

GLØGG (MULLED WINE)

Most northern European countries have a recipe for mulled wine or gluhwein; what sets Danish gløgg apart is the addition of the slivered almonds and raisins that can be eaten with a spoon once you get to the bottom of the glass. Many recipes will encourage you to use expensive wine, but to be honest you're going to put so many other spices and flavours in that I would save your good bottle for later on in the evening.

Ingredients

- 750ml bottle of wine
- 8 cardamom pods
- 1 cinnamon stick
- 5 cloves
- 150g raisins
- 50g flaked almonds
- 1 orange
- 200g brown sugar
- 250ml port
- 125ml of brandy or akvavit (optional)

1. Pare the rind from the orange using a potato peeler so it is in large strips, avoiding the bitter white pith.

2. Put the wine, spices, raisins, almonds, sugar and rind in a large saucepan and place on a low heat. The aim is to warm it slowly enough that the sugar dissolves and the spices permeate the wine, but not heat it up so much that the alcohol begins to evaporate.

3. After thirty minutes, stir in the brandy/akvavit and port, bring back up to a nice low simmer and then serve in tall glasses with a spoon, ensuring each one has a dollop of nuts and fruit at the bottom.

HOME-MADE AKVAVIT

A hyggelig festive party season, as we have seen, is largely based around the provision of huge quantities of mouth-watering food; however, there is one other element which adds a certain indefinable element of joy to a social gathering, and that is the tradition of akvavit. Danish snaps is defined as a spirit infused with fruits, botanicals or other more bonkers ingredients (liquorice pipe snaps, anyone?) and is often flavoured in the home, whereas akvavit is a snaps predominantly flavoured with dill or caraway, produced by distilleries.

The first references to akvavit date to around the 1500s, when herbs and spices were added to raw alcohol to cover its rough taste. I grew up drinking Aalborg akvavit, which has smooth aniseedy overtones, but as it can be hard to source outside of Denmark this is my version. No family party can go by without just 'en lille én', or just 'a little one'... more than three and one will need to reserve a place on the sofa for the night. Skål!

Ingredients

- 500ml grain-based vodka
- 1tsp caraway seeds
- 1 star anise
- 1 tsp coriander seeds
- ½tsp dried dill, or a sprig of fresh
- ½tsp fennel seeds
- An orange

1. Sterilise a large, wide mouth glass jar and pour in the vodka. When making heavily flavoured snaps with lots of sugar in, I tend to use cheaper vodkas; however, as this recipe doesn't have that quantity of sweetness, I think it is worth using a better quality bottle for making akvavit.

2. Peel two long strips of peel from the orange, avoiding the bitter white pith, and place in the jar along with all the other herbs and spices.

3. Leave overnight, removing the orange peel and star anise after twenty-four hours. Keep it on the kitchen counter and shake it every time you walk past it.

4. On the third day, have a little taste; if the flavour is already strong enough for your liking, strain the vodka through a paper coffee filter, kitchen paper or muslin to remove the herbs; otherwise leave in a dark cupboard and keep tasting it for up to two weeks until you are satisfied with its fresh, green herbiness before straining (I find five days is perfect).

5. To serve, pop the bottle in the freezer a couple of hours before you need it; sip it ice cold from tiny glasses with a lager chaser, looking your drinking-partner in the eye and toasting frequently.

WOLF'S BEST EVER HOT CHOCOLATE

Ever selfless, my son and I have spent a great deal of time experimenting with many different hot chocolate recipes over the last few winters, and now, slightly more than two stone heavier, I bring you our absolute favourite. Indulgently thick and silky, it has a continental feel to it, reminiscent of dipping churros into chocolate. Containing, as it does, two bars of dark chocolate, it is very rich, so we tend to drink it in small cups; if you can't find a fresh churros stall nearby, we have found sponge fingers a particularly effective substitute for dunking.

Ingredients

- 2 x 100g bars of dark 70 per cent chocolate
- 100g icing sugar
- 100g cocoa
- 50g cornflour
- Pinch of sea salt
- Pinch of cinnamon
- Milk, approx. 200ml per serving.

1. Chill the chocolate bars in the fridge for twenty minutes and then blitz in a food processor.

2. When reduced to a crumb-like texture, add all the other dry ingredients and whizz to combine thoroughly, then tip into a glass storage jar.

3. To make the hot chocolate, simply pour 200ml of milk per person into a saucepan, and add two large heaped tablespoons of the mixture for each serving.

4. Bring to a simmer and whisk for about five minutes until all the chocolate has melted and the mixture has thickened to a beautifully creamy texture. At this point I like to add an extra pinch of cinnamon and a hefty glug of rum (not for the kids), before serving in little cups or mulled wine beakers.

CHAPTER FIVE

FAMILY FUN

PAKKELEG

Pakkeleg (meaning 'package game') is a traditional Danish party game played at Christmas. Suitable for grown-ups as well as kids, it is perfect for those families who enjoy a good-natured festive bicker, especially after a couple of drinks. Each guest brings a small wrapped gift (usually something cheap and cheerful like sweeties or a joke present) and you will also need dice and a timer.

How to play

Round 1. Everybody starts by placing a small wrapped gift in the centre of the table. Players each take a turn to roll the dice once; if a 6 is thrown, they may take a gift, then the play moves on until all the presents have been removed.

Round 2. Set a time limit (we generally go for 1 minute). Each player now has that amount of allotted time to roll the dice continuously and score as many 6s possible. Every 6 entitles them to steal a gift from another player. If a 3 is rolled, all gifts are passed to the person seated to the left, and if a 1 is rolled, you can steal a gift from anyone around the table and give it to someone else (you would think that everyone would be generous and give it to the person who has nothing, but that rarely happens).

Once everyone has had a turn, all the presents are opened. Held og lykke (good luck!).

GRÅDIG (GREEDY DICE)

I have an old film canister stuffed with tiny dice which I have been carrying around in my pocket since I was back-packing in my twenties, and it has been invaluable ever since, turning both long waits at airports and rainy evenings at the pub into a jolly experience.

'Greedy' is one of our favourite games, and is perfect for keeping everyone entertained after dinner, especially with a little glass of liqueur and some dark chocolates on the side. There is also a most enjoyable element of risk involved as you can either decide to stick safely on your score or risk going higher and losing it all.

Five dice are thrown, and as long as you keep scoring on every throw, you can keep rolling and accumulating more points. Fail to score and you lose everything from that turn. The object is to be the first player to score 10,000 points, however, you need to roll at least 400 from one turn to be able to enter the game.

How to play

1. Player one rolls five dice. Scoring dice are set aside and the others are rolled again. If all five dice end up scoring then all five can be rolled again.

2. Only 1s and 5s count by themselves and can be set aside on their own. Other numbers can only be counted in another scoring combination (such as four of a kind).

3. To enter the game, the player must roll at least 400 points, which is recorded on the score sheet.

4. The player may stop at any point and stick on their score; they may also choose to save just some of their scoring dice, and roll the others if they wish.

5. If no scoring dice or combinations are rolled then any score is lost, the turn is ended and play passes to the next person.

6. When one player reaches 10,000 (although you may wish to make it less if there are lots of players), every other player takes one more turn in order to try and pip them at post.

Scoring combinations

One 1=100 points
Two 1s=200 points
Three 1s=1000 points
One 5=50 points
Two 5s=100 points
Three 5s=500 points

Three of a kind

Three 2s=200 points
Three 3s=300 points
Three 4s=400 points
Three 5s=500 points
Three 6s=600 points

Four of a kind (e.g. four 5s)

1,250 points

Five of a kind (e.g. five 5s)

1,500 points

A Straight (e.g. 2,3,4,5,6 or 1,2,3,4,5)

2,000 points

A Full House (e.g. two 3s and three 5s)

2,500 points

THE CANDY CANE GAME

While I do love a quiz at Christmas, there comes a point during every party where entertainment of a less cerebral nature becomes appropriate. The Candy Cane Game ticks all the boxes for festive fun; kids love it, you can make the rules as simple or as complicated as you like, and up to thirteen people can play with just one pack of cards.

The easiest way to explain it is as a game of Musical Chairs, using sweets instead of chairs, and cards instead of music. The objective is to get four of a kind and swipe a candy cane, and thus avoid being the last person left without one.

1. Lay the candy canes on the table, ensuring there is one cane fewer than the number of players; hence five players will require four canes. Move any glasses or candles out of the way (you'll thank me later). If you don't have any candy canes, spoons make a good alternative).

2. Choose one person as the dealer, who then deals each player four cards. Any leftover cards become his draw pile.

3. The dealer draws a card, looks at it and then discards one from his hand of five to the player on his left, before drawing another from the pile, looking at and discarding again; he should keep drawing and discarding as fast as possible.

4. Meanwhile the player to his left looks at his hand of five and then discards one to his left, and so on. Keep playing as fast as you can; inevitably there will be a blockage with one person taking much longer to make decisions, and at this point it is perfectly acceptable to bellow at them impatiently.

5. The last player puts all his thrown away cards on a discard pile, which can then be shuffled and used by the dealer if his draw pile runs out.

6. If any player manages to get four of a kind, they can take a candy cane; they might wish to do this as sneakily as possible, or indeed make a huge fuss about it, but the choice is theirs.

7. Now all the other players must grab a candy cane; the person left without one now has to sit out.

8. You cannot touch a cane until the person with four of a kind has actually picked up theirs; if you do, the round ends and you are out; hence there is a lot of possibility for 'fake-grabbing', particularly by the more annoying members of the party.

9. The dealership moves along one player for the next round, and a candy cane is taken away so there is always one fewer than the number of players remaining. Play continues until there is just one triumphant victor.

Variations in rules can be endless, and will no doubt change every time you play it. One rule which is particular to our family is that yes, a broken cane can be eaten, but only by the people who didn't break it in the first place. If you have more players, just add in another pack of cards. Jokers can be used as wild cards, and if you really want to bring an extra layer of chaos to your party, put the candy canes in a different room.

TEMPLATES

Kravlenisser (literally 'crawling pixies'') are more accurately described as 'shelf-pixies'. The first drawings were originally designed by cartoonist Frederik Bramming in the 1940s and they are usually purchased in printed-out sheets, to be cut out with scissors at home. Each pixie has a little paper tab that can be tucked under a book or taped to a shelf, and they are usually indulging in some sort of miscreant behaviour.

I thought it might be rather fun to include some in this book, so I do hope you photocopy them for your family to cut out and colour in!

JULEHJERTER TEMPLATE

SUPPLIERS

Scandikitchen
www.scandikitchen.co.uk
Suppliers of baking ingredients and all sorts of lovely Nordic foods

Creativ Company
www.cc-craft.co.uk
Craft and hobby supplies

Star Child Glastonbury
www.starchild.co.uk
Essential oils and dried herbs, bottles and jars

Musgrove Willows
www.musgrovewillows.co.uk
Suppliers of willow withies, tools and kits

Hygge Style
www.hyggestyle.co.uk
Danish Christmas essentials, craft kits and paper star strips